REA

362.
Berkman,
The HMO survival guide

ACPL ITEM
DISCARDED

☞ S0-BWV-415

ALLEN COUNTY PUBLIC LIBRARY
FORT WAYNE, INDIANA 46802

You may return this book to any location of
the Allen County Public Library.

DEMCO

THE
HMO
SURVIVAL
GUIDE

Save Money, Play by the Rules,
and Get the Best Care

SUE BERKMAN

VILLARD / NEW YORK

Kern County Public Library
900 Webster Street
PO Box 2270
Bakersfield, CA

Neither the author of *The HMO Survival Guide* nor the publisher takes responsibility for possible consequences from any treatment, procedure, application of medication or preparation, or action by any person reading or following the information in this book. *The HMO Survival Guide* is intended as an informational resource and does not attempt to replace your physician, pharmacist, or other health care provider. The author of *The HMO Survival Guide* attests to the accuracy of the material contained herein insofar as such information was available at the time of publication. Neither the author nor the publisher attests to or endorses the quality of services of the various agencies mentioned in *The HMO Survival Guide*.

Copyright © 1997 by Sue Berkman

All rights reserved under International and Pan-American Copyright Conventions. Published in the United States by Villard Books, a division of Random House, Inc., New York, and simultaneously in Canada by Random House of Canada Limited, Toronto.

VILLARD BOOKS is a registered trademark of Random House, Inc.

Library of Congress Cataloging-in-Publication Data

Berkman, Sue.
The HMO survival guide: save money, play by the rules, and get the best care / Sue Berkman.
p.   cm.
ISBN 0-679-77816-0
1. Health maintenance organizations—Popular works.   2. Consumer education.   I. Title.
RA413.B47   1998
362.1'04258—dc21   97-36701

Random House website address: www.randomhouse.com
Printed in the United States of America on acid-free paper
24689753
First Edition
Book Design by Jo Anne Metsch

ACKNOWLEDGMENTS

In the process of writing this book, I received both good advice and invaluable information from many sources, including The Commonwealth Fund, Opinion Research International, the National Consumers League, the Public Advocate for the City of New York, the American Medical Association, Group Health Association of America, Interstudy, and *Managed Care Marketing*.

I am most grateful for the time and unwavering concern of the many health care consumers who were willing to share their ideas and experiences in the hope and belief that such networking will benefit others.

At Villard, my gratitude goes to Craig Nelson, the editor who recognized the need for a guide to the intricate workings of HMOs, and to Melissa Milsten, whose special editing skills and good sense brought the manuscript to its present form.

My special thanks to my agent, Barbara Lowenstein, for her support and encouragement.

And a special thanks to the many others who offered motivation and reassurance along the way.

CONTENTS

PART I

WELCOME
TO THE WORLD
OF HMOs

ONE

IN SICKNESS AND IN HEALTH

DO YOU THINK IT COULDN'T HAPPEN TO YOU?

• A four-year-old girl undergoes a routine tonsillectomy in a New York City hospital. She shows no apparent problems in the recovery room and is sent home the same day, as directed by her HMO. During the night she begins to bleed profusely and is rushed to the emergency room and then hospitalized. She dies four days later.

• A woman undergoes a routine Pap smear, which comes back normal from the laboratory hired by her HMO. Three days later, another Pap test shows that she has advanced cervical cancer. An investigation of medical and laboratory records shows that the cancer cells in three Pap smears and three biopsies went unrecognized.

• A nine-year-old girl is diagnosed with a rare form of kidney cancer requiring surgery. Her family's HMO refuses to allow a pediatric specialist to perform the operation, insisting that it be done by the HMO's own doctors. The child's family goes ahead with the specialist and is left with a $50,000 bill to pay on their own.

• Following elective surgery at a California hospital that is part of an HMO, a man begins to hemorrhage internally. For over an hour and a half, he remains unchecked by the hospital's nursing staff. He dies on his forty-seventh birthday.

• A thirty-year-old woman needs surgery to have a spinal tumor removed. Her HMO tells her that payment will be denied unless the operation is performed by one of their approved surgeons—even though the doctor has never performed this surgery before. The HMO stands by its decision even when an experienced doctor offers to perform the surgery without a fee.

THE NEW GUARDIANS OF HEALTH CARE

In the past fifteen years, Americans have lived through an upheaval in the rules governing health care. Today, there's a whole conglomeration of authorities—government, industry, health plans, health insurers—who not only pay the bills for medical treatment but now insist on having a say in how that medical treatment is offered and even whether it should be offered at all. These efficiency experts are changing the business of medicine or, more precisely, changing medicine into a business—a business called managed care.

Right now, in fact, 72 percent of American workers are enrolled in wholly or partly managed plans of one kind or another, ranging from health maintenance organizations (HMOs) to traditional health insurance programs with a new look. If you count yourself in that number, you probably recognize certain characteristics that are common to your own plan and your neighbor's plan. For example:

• You are required to choose a primary care doctor who will act as your *gatekeeper*, evaluating your medical complaints and either treating them or referring you to a specialist or hospital.

• You are limited in your choice of primary care doctor to an approved listing issued by the health care plan you belong to. The listing includes internists, family practitioners, and pediatricians—specialties that are most often considered to be gener-alists—and, for women, obstetricians and gynecologists.

• You are offered a range of preventive care services such as frequent checkups and health screenings so that minor ail-ments may be caught early enough to be cured with inexpen-sive treatments and even serious conditions may be diagnosed early enough to be treated more effectively.

• You are offered medical care and hospital services but probably not to the extent of the traditional insurance plans you have been covered by in the past.

• You are not required to file medical claim forms because the HMO pays your doctor, hospital, or other health care provider directly. However, you may be expected to pay a small copay-ment (typically about $10, but sometimes as little as $5 and even as much as $15) at the time of your office visit.

• Every month or two, or perhaps once a year, you pay a pre-mium, a fixed fee that covers all your medical care for the com-ing year. If you work for a company, your employer probably pays part of the fee and you share in the cost. If you are self-employed, you pay the entire premium yourself.

• If you choose to receive medical care from a provider who is not part of your plan's network, you will have to bear the cost of most—if not all—of that care on your own.

For all their common characteristics, HMOs vary widely. Consequently, your experiences with your own HMO may be different from your neighbor's or those of your neighbor's neighbor. These differences have to do with variations not only in the plans themselves, but also in each individual's way of participating in them.

WHY YOU NEED THIS BOOK

Right now, if you are a member of an HMO or about to join one and you don't have the right information, you are virtually powerless to stand up for yourself in the face of all the many potential hurdles. This book will give you the power to overcome them by revealing the inner workings of HMOs in general and, probably, your HMO in particular.

- This is a cautionary tale of how managed care got started in the first place and how, once the ball got rolling, it was impossible to stop.
- This is an exposé of the necessary facts that don't show up in any marketing brochure.
- This is a handbook that will make it simpler to get over and around the obstacles to maintaining your health care.

The material included has been selected based on the understanding that most people are fairly easy-going about their health care until they become sick or feel that they are being misguided.

HOW TO READ THIS BOOK

There are three basic parts to this book:

Part I, "Welcome to the World of HMOs," reviews and explains the growth of managed care and compares and contrasts managed care with traditional insurance.

Part II, "What You Should Know About Your HMO That It Would Rather You Didn't," explains the difference between profit and not-for-profit and why it matters. It also reveals how a doctor's payment affects your care, tells how to determine if a doctor is really available, considers the situation of doctors withholding facts that may be crucial to your well-being, describes the limits to hospital care and treatment for psychological problems, gives a peek at the advertising budgets of the major managed care organizations as well as the exorbitant salaries paid to some top executives, and finally, provides assurance that the law is behind you.

Part III, "What You Should Do to Get the Most from Your HMO," assumes that you belong among the 72 percent of the population who are already enrolled in some form of managed care plan. This section gives an invaluable collection of tools to ensure you receive the best care possible, with tips on how to pick a superior doctor, how to choose the right plan, how to learn your rights, how to protect your privacy, how to save money, how to get your HMO to say "yes" when it has said "no," how to file a complaint, how to deal with uncommon issues, and how to solicit alternative treatments and have them paid for.

It is not essential to have read Part I before beginning to gather your ammunition from Part II or putting your resources to work in Part III. The sooner you begin, the better.

TWO

THE HMO REVOLUTION

FROM MODEST BEGINNINGS TO MEGAMERGERS

Billion-dollar managed care consolidations . . . marriages of convenience between hospitals . . . mutinous doctors . . . angry patients . . . horror-story headlines. How did our current state of health care develop from a modest attempt to provide Americans with a simple and cost-effective way to take care of themselves?

The pioneering event occurred in 1929, when the Los Angeles Department of Water and Power offered its two thousand employees and their families a managed care plan. A contractual agreement was arranged with two doctors who, in exchange for a prepaid monthly fee of a few dollars, would provide the plan's participants with essential medical services and hospital facilities.

Similar health plans became operative during the Depression years when financial need forced many medical practitioners to join in group practice and community clinics sponsored by trade unions, fraternal organizations, and consumer advocates. In the 1940s, the not-for-profit Health Insurance Plan (HIP) was introduced in New York City (for more information on profit and not-for-profit plans, see page 29). As HIP evolved and flourished, it became the model for many later and larger groups.

For the country as a whole, managed care began its gradual move to center stage in 1969, the year that the National Governors' Association put its weight behind a federal proposal to contain escalating costs of health care through a different kind of insurance. Four years later, during the Nixon presidency, the proposal was passed into law as the Health Maintenance Organization Act. Its basic requirement was that an enterprise employing twenty-five or more people had to offer its employees a prepaid managed health care package as an alternative to traditional health insurance. Managed care plans have varied widely (and wildly) from this original concept. Yet the name HMO has stuck to this day.

TAKING OFF . . . AND OVER

The HMO movement took a few years to develop momentum but eventually replaced what was long accepted as the health care "industry." In 1976, about 175 managed care plans were on record; twenty years later, the count was up to 591 and increasing almost daily. The number of people enrolled in HMOs in 1980 was a modest 9 million; by 1996, more than 58 million Americans—one fifth of this country's population—had signed on. This phenomenal spurt in growth was fed by employers' voracious appetite for ways to cut the skyrocketing costs of health care benefits. Because managed care has proved to be a money-saving move, it is now offered to employees of 81 percent of all businesses.

IT'S STILL LIKE WALKING ON SHIFTING SAND

Keeping up with HMOs is no easy matter. Over the years, they have been conforming to consumer demands and government regulations. They now typically grant more freedom to patients and professional health providers. Newer groups organized by doctors for their own profit tend to remain small and local; on the other hand, many older, more established organizations are now all over the map as they join forces with major insurance companies and provide megabucks for investors. The HMO that covers your health care today may be quite different tomorrow.

There's little doubt that HMOs have accomplished their primary goal of significantly reducing the cost of the nation's health care. This has been achieved by cutting down on permissible visits to expensive specialists, placing strict limits on the use of new high-tech tests and other costly diagnostic tools, encouraging outpatient clinic treatment instead of hospitalization for simpler surgical procedures, and shortening hospital stays for more serious operations.

BUT AT WHAT PRICE?

Doctors and other health care providers warned, early on, that the industry's efforts to maintain an acceptable bottom line would be achieved at the expense of patients' well-being, especially in four situations:

- When patients are too frequently discouraged from consulting with specialists;
- When coverage for emergency treatment is inadequate and may even be withheld;
- When patients are discharged from hospitals "quicker and sicker";
- When patients' mental health problems are not properly diagnosed and treated and when confidentiality regarding these problems is breached.

Many patients contend that this scenario has come true.

AND REAL DOLLARS ON TOP OF THAT

Most people join an HMO through their place of employment, just as they typically acquire indemnity insurance plans.

Though in the past the employer was almost always responsible for every employee's whole health care, the cost of paying for HMO care is split between the two. Premiums vary by location. Workers in big cities usually pay more than those in small towns. A survey by KPMG/Peat Marwick found that a typical annual premium for an individual is under $3,500; for a family, the premium increases to about $5,000. And it all comes out of your paycheck before you even realize it is gone. That's before you even see a doctor, which will add on another $5 to $15 per visit.

THREE

THE "NEW WAY" VERSUS THE "OLD WAY"

GET READY FOR A CHANGE—IT MAY NOT BE EASY

A majority of readers probably fit this example: You've been covered by health insurance for one, five, ten, or even more years. For all or most of that time, you've worked for someone else, who has provided insurance as part of your employment package. You've pretty much taken for granted that the cost of your health care would be covered by your policy, and your involvement has been limited to filling out forms after receiving treatment. If you counted yourself among the smaller number that pays for its own health insurance, you chose a policy based primarily on its hospitalization benefits, knowing a hospital stay could wipe you out financially.

Did you know that the traditional type of insurance is called indemnity insurance and, sometimes, fee-for-service insurance? Did you know that you are, in fact, paying for every treatment, because each one adds to the total cost of the nation's health care and this in turn affects the cost of health insurance for each individual employer, which in turn may affect your pay scale? Do you know, in fact, that you played a vital role in sending the cost of health care skyrocketing to more than $1 trillion in 1994?

If you have remained unaware of all of the above, it will be difficult to understand the inner workings of managed care because you have little or no basis for comparison. So here, in a neat package, is a summary comparison of HMO coverage versus indemnity insurance in terms of the most important issues in health care coverage.

INDEMNITY INSURERS VERSUS HMOs

WHAT THEY ARE

Indemnity insurance provides coverage for loss. When used to describe traditional health care insurance it suggests coverage for loss of health.

Health Maintenance Organizations are organized health care plans that provide and pay for comprehensive health care services for an enrolled group of members in a specific area. HMOs manage medical care for their enrollees.

CHOOSING A DOCTOR

Indemnity insurance allows you to make your own decisions about when to consult a doctor and who to consult. You are free to decide when you want a second opinion. For major surgery coverage, second opinions are often required. You may also choose to consult alternative therapists from time to time.

HMOs put restrictions on choice of doctors. In the most restrictive type, known as the Staff/Group Model, where providers are all located within a single facility, you are expected to consult only those doctors and other health providers who have a contractual affiliation with the plan. In less restrictive types such as Independent Practice Associations (IPAs), where doctors practice in their private offices, you may go "outside the network" but will have to pay more than the usual copayment.

CHOOSING A SPECIALIST

Indemnity insurance allows you to make appointments with doctors on your own, although such consultations usually happen with your regular doctor as a go-between.

HMOs restrict you to the use of a specialist within the organization's network of doctors and even then only with the referral of your primary care doctor. This means that you can't select and schedule an appointment with a specialist such as a dermatologist or rheumatologist on your own. If referral is withheld, you have the option of appealing the decision or of consulting an outside specialist with the understanding that you will be responsible for a higher percentage—or maybe all—of the charges. If you're not familiar with referrals, turn to page 47 to find out the two reasons why your doctor would send you to another doctor.

TYPE OF CARE

Indemnity insurance does not cover the cost of most health care that is considered "preventive," including screenings and routine medical checkups. This type of insurance is largely limited to treatment of illness.

HMOs cover the cost of routine medical checkups and preventive health care, including health screenings and even some kinds of alternative treatments. This type of insurance covers treatment of illness but emphasizes preventive measures to avoid illness.

HOSPITAL ADMISSIONS

Indemnity insurance generally covers hospital procedures and stay, whether you are to be hospitalized for an elective procedure or for an emergency. The hospital is usually determined by the doctor who is to perform the procedure.

HMOs limit your hospitalizations to those institutions that are part of the network. Going to a hospital outside the network because of an emergency or while traveling is rarely covered by the HMO contract.

PAYMENT

Indemnity insurance allows for reimbursement of your direct payments to a doctor (usually 80 percent of your up-front payment) after you have satisfied a yearly deductible amount (which may be as little as $200 or over $1,000). Sometimes the doctor will bill the insurance company directly, which relieves the burden of paying for treatment.

HMOs usually don't hold you responsible for a deductible or, at worst, include a very small one. You pay only a slight charge, or copayment, of $5 to $15 each time you visit one of the doctors in the plan. Copayments are also required for inpatient and outpatient services at the hospitals in the HMO network. You may or may not be reimbursed for money spent on emergency treatment or for professional care during travel. You may not be reimbursed for more than a specified number of sessions with a mental health professional. (If you want to know more about coverage for mental health, see page 52.)

CLAIM FORMS

Indemnity insurance puts the responsibility on you to complete claim forms in conjunction with your doctor. You are responsible for following up on payments and must call the insurance company if your reimbursement check is delayed.

HMOs take the burden off you and put it squarely on the shoulders of your doctor.

QUALITY OF CARE

Indemnity insurance does not carry responsibility for the quality of care for members because doctors and other health care providers are chosen by the individual member.

HMOs are responsible for the quality of care received by its members.

PART II

WHAT YOU SHOULD KNOW ABOUT YOUR HMO THAT IT WOULD RATHER YOU DIDN'T

PICK A MODEL, ANY MODEL

THERE ARE MANY WAYS TO BUILD AN HMO

HMOs come in a variety of forms, or "models." Each one has its own advantages and disadvantages.

- The *Group Model HMO* signs a contract with one or more groups of doctors, whose services are available to patients in the same plan. In some Group HMOs, participating doctors may treat only those patients who are that plan's members. Although the core of such HMOs usually consists of family practitioners, multispecialty groups are often part of the same picture and are located on the same premises. The group is paid on a capitated basis, which means that a set fee is established by the HMO for each patient regardless of how much or how little care is provided. Doctors are paid on a fee-for-service basis.

  + Premiums are lower than with indemnity plans.
  + Out-of-pocket expenses are lower than with indemnity plans.
  + Doctors have wider selection of specialists in affiliated groups for referrals.

+ Doctors work out of their own offices.
+ Doctors have no financial incentive to decrease services.
+ Doctors have some financial incentive to use full services.
− There is limited flexibility in choosing providers.

A few HMOs based on this model are Fallon Community Health Plan, Massachusetts; Harvard Community Health Plan, Massachusetts; and Group Health Cooperative of Puget Sound, Washington.

• The *Independent Practice Association* (IPA) includes large numbers of independent doctors who are in private practice. These doctors are paid a fixed fee for treating IPA members but they can also treat patients who are not members of the plan. This type of organization most closely resembles the traditional indemnity insurance, which is probably why it has become so popular among patients and so well advertised among managed care organizations that want to solicit new members.

+ Doctors work out of their own offices.
+ This type may feel less like an HMO than other types of managed care plans.
+ There is wider choice of primary care doctors.
+ There is wider choice of specialists.
− There may be less control over the quality of service provided by each individual doctor.

A few HMOs based on this model are Oxford Health Plans; MVP Health Plan, New York; Community Health Plan, New York; Harris Methodist Health Plan, Texas; and Care America Health Plans, California.

• The *Network Model HMO* tries to be all things to all people. It offers some Group model components and some

IPA components. The downside of this is that you are never really sure of the rules of the game—if in fact there are any.

Multispecialty groups of doctors have contracts with more than one HMO and may also have patients with traditional insurance coverage.

+ Doctors practice in their individual offices.
+ There is a wider choice of primary care doctors.
+ There is a wider choice of specialists.
− There may be less control over the quality of service provided by each individual doctor.

A few HMOs based on this model are CIGNA HealthCare; FHP; HealthAmerica Pennsylvania; PacifiCare of California; and Aetna/U.S. Healthcare.

• The *Preferred Provider Organization* (PPO) pays doctors for services as they are rendered but at prearranged rates. This assures discounted, uniform fees, as opposed to fee-for-service plans in which charges for identical services can vary from doctor to doctor. PPO members may go to the plan's doctors or get care outside the network. PPO doctors may provide care for patients who are not members of the plan.

+ It is not required that health care be coordinated by a primary care doctor.
+ There is more flexibility in seeing specialists and out-of-network doctors.
− It is usually more expensive than other types.
− There may be restrictions on preexisting conditions.

• The *Exclusive Provider Organization* (EPO) offers the same payment procedures as a PPO. Members must get medical care from EPO doctors only, and doctors may only treat patients who are members of the plan.

+ Members can get care without authorization from a primary care doctor.

- Costs are greater than with traditional HMOs.
- All care is limited to EPO providers.

• The *Physician-Hospital Organization* (PHO) is an organized group of doctors who are affiliated with a particular hospital and provide services to patients who enroll in their plan as they would in an HMO.

+ Members have wide choice of primary care doctors, specialists, and hospitals.
+ Cost is less than traditional indemnity insurance.
- Cost is higher than traditional HMOs.

FREEDOM OF CHOICE: POINT OF SERVICE

A *Point of Service Plan* (POS) is not technically an HMO, but rather is an option that is offered by any kind of HMO—Group, IPA, or Network Model combination—and it puts the HMO somewhere between a standard HMO and traditional indemnity insurance with regard to benefits, coverage, and cost. Simply put, the POS plan means that you can choose to get care from doctors and hospitals outside the network and still be covered, at least in part. If you stay "in network," you receive care from the HMO's network of doctors and hospitals and will pay no deductibles but only small visit fees as long as care is provided or arranged by your primary doctor. If you go "out of network," you will share a larger part of the cost for your care by paying a deductible (which can range from a few hundred to a thousand dollars) and then paying a higher percentage of the actual cost of care. But—and this is what is so important to many people who are used to indemnity insurance—you can continue to visit your own family doctor, see your favorite gynecologist, keep your chosen pediatrician—and the cost will be covered, at least to some degree.

WHICH HMO IS FOR YOU?

Before you spend too much time trying to figure out which of the above HMO or non-HMO plans to join, you should find out what is available to you.

If you work for someone else, your choice will be limited by what your employer provides, although many employers offer at least a limited selection of plans.

If you work for yourself, your choice may be limited by what you can afford.

If you own a small business, you may be able to join with other small business owners.

If you are retired, you must adhere to the type of coverage offered by the government.

MAKING THE MOST OF YOUR HMO PLAN

The nation's managed care organizations would have you believe that they act as a beneficent parent, making sure that your every health need is attended to, completely and in a timely fashion. The nation's doctors and other health care providers would have you believe that managed care companies make it impossible for them to do their job properly and that you will suffer the worst for it. Who should you believe?

While millions of Americans have been well served and cared for by HMOs, many have been inconvenienced and frustrated by the new rules—and some people have gotten sicker or even died because of too little care or bad care. Surveys by the Department of Health and Human Services and the Group Health Association of America show that patient satisfaction ranges from 75 percent in top-rated HMOs to less than 35 percent in lowest-rated HMOs. How can you position yourself solidly among the millions who are well served? Since the best defense is a good offense, it's in your best interest to check out an HMO before checking in.

General Facts You Need to Know Before Joining an HMO

If you are going to make any health-care-related choice, make sure it is an informed one. As you begin to compare the HMOs, there are a number of sources you should consult, including:

• *Employer benefits manager.* The benefits manager in your place of work should have samples of member materials and should share them with you. This individual can also tell you how many employees in your own company have signed up with a specific HMO.

• *HMO informational packages.* The marketing material available to consumers who have not yet enrolled is more generalized than the materials sent to new enrollees. However, any kind of written material will give you a sense of how much importance the plan places on communication with its members.

• *HMO member services or customer relations divisions.* You can request a new-member package, but it is unlikely that you will receive it if you are not a member. In any case, the service representatives are prepared to answer certain questions, such as the ones listed below, which you should ask before making any decision.

1. Does this plan cover the following basic preventive services?
   Immunizations for children   Yes __ No __ Copay __
   Immunizations for adults   Yes __ No __ Copay __
   Mammography   Yes __ No __ Copay __
   PAP test   Yes __ No __ Copay __
   Colon cancer screening   Yes __ No __ Copay __
   Blood pressure screening   Yes __ No __ Copay __
   Cholesterol screening   Yes __ No __ Copay __
   Routine physical exam   Yes __ No __ Copay __
   Eye and ear exams   Yes __ No __ Copay __
   Well baby exams   Yes __ No __ Copay __
2. Is there a yearly deductible?   Yes __ No __ Copay __
3. Are there coverage limits for chronic problems?   Yes __ No __ Copay __
4. Is there a maximum coverage limit?   Yes __ No __ Copay __

5. Does the plan restrict
   preexisting conditions?   Yes __ No __ Copay __
6. Does the plan cover
   alternative therapies?   Yes __ No __ Copay __
7. Does the plan cover
   experimental therapies?   Yes __ No __ Copay __
8. Does the plan cover maternity
   services?   Yes __ No __ Copay __
9. Does the plan cover mental
   health services?   Yes __ No __ Copay __
10. Does the plan cover alcohol
    and drug addiction treatment?   Yes __ No __ Copay __
11. Does the plan include
    hospitalization?   Yes __ No __ Copay __
12. Does the plan cover emergency
    care away from home?   Yes __ No __ Copay __
13. How long has the HMO been
    in business?   _____ years
14. What percentage of doctors
    are board certified?   _____ percent
15. Are there restrictions on
    choosing doctors?   Yes __ No __ Limits __
16. Does the plan allow for
    changing doctors?   Yes __ No __ Limits __
17. Does the plan restrict choice
    of hospital?   Yes __ No __ Limits __
18. What type of HMO is this?   Group __ IPA __ Network __
19. Is this HMO part of a
    nationwide HMO?   Yes __ No __
20. Is this HMO approved by a
    state agency?   Yes __ No __
    What is the agency's name?   _____

Specific Facts to Know Before Joining

Health care is different for men, women, children, and seniors. By asking the right questions, you can get the kind of care that optimizes your health.

1. Are there doctors in the HMO who specialize in women's, men's, children's, and seniors' health?   Yes __ No __
2. Does the primary care doctor coordinate care with specialists?   Yes __ No __
3. Does the HMO offer special classes in women's, men's, children's, and seniors' health?   Yes __ No __
4. Does the plan allow for preventive screenings for high-risk situations such as family history of cancer or heart disease?   Yes __ No __
5. Does the plan make allowances for religious or cultural concerns?   Yes __ No __
6. Does the primary care doctor allow patient participation in the decision-making process when diagnosing or planning treatments?   Yes __ No __

YOUR FAMILY PORTRAIT

Before choosing an HMO you should estimate the expected, predictable health care needs of each family member over the next year. You can do this by reviewing your medical records for the past several years. If you have not kept copies of your medical records (don't worry, you are not alone), how do you get copies of them? Turn now to Chapter 9, page 59, for a step-by-step process. While answers to the items below will not tell you which plan is best for your family, they can point you in the right direction and help you estimate your health care costs over the next year. You should then compare your estimated costs to the various plans and see which plan is likely to provide the best service and which will be the better financial deal.

Once you have your medical records in hand, here are some points to consider:

1. How many visits to the doctor have there been for preventive services such as childhood immunizations?
2. How many visits to the doctor are expected for preventive services such as mammograms, Pap tests, or sigmoidoscopies?
3. If you are a woman, are you planning to become pregnant and deliver in the next year?
4. Do you have a chronic condition, such as diabetes, that requires ongoing medical care and medication?
5. Do you tend to go to the doctor for minor problems that might clear up on their own?
6. Do you practice medical self-care to avoid going to the physician?
7. What was the average cost for health care for you and your family each year?
8. Is your family healthy?
9. Do you have habits like smoking or excessive drinking that may compromise your health?
10. Are you sedentary or do you exercise regularly?

What You Can Do Once You Are In an HMO

Even after you have joined an HMO, you can protect yourself against unnecessary frustration and, worse, bad health care.

Switch doctors if necessary. If the primary care physician whom you thought was so perfect after your assessment of credentials and your first encounter is providing cursory care or even discouraging care altogether, you shouldn't waste time finding a new doctor. Call the HMO's member service or customer relations department, state your problem clearly, and ask how to go about changing doctors. Most plans make it easy to switch physicians at any time and as many times as you wish, although you should bear in mind that while you are shopping for a new doctor you might be missing out on vital medical attention.

SWITCHING DOCTORS

The service manager will want to know why you are dissatisfied with your doctor. Is there one reason or are there a number of them? Here are some reasons why most people want to switch doctors.

1. The doctor was abrupt and unfriendly.
2. The doctor didn't explain the diagnosis.
3. The doctor was late for the scheduled appointment.
4. The doctor didn't explain the medication.
5. The doctor discussed the case with the office staff.
6. The doctor's office staff was unpleasant.

Switch plans if you are really dissatisfied and if you can. Many employers offer a choice of at least two HMOs, and you should be ready at the next open enrollment. If you are enrolled on your own, investigate the various plans available in your region and repeat the review process itemized above.

Set aside funds for care that you think you need and that your HMO won't pay for. You can certainly appeal the denial, but in the meantime you need to have your health care needs met and you may have to pay out of pocket to do so.

Check out the HMO's track record with your state regulatory agency to determine what its past history has been with regard to denial of payments. A listing of state agencies that regulate HMOs (as well as doctors and hospitals) is in Appendix A, page 103.

Be a squeaky wheel about lack of services, denial of care, or for that matter, anything that bothers you about your HMO. You don't want to be a chronic complainer, but if you don't tell them, how will they know?

FIVE

TO PROFIT OR NOT TO PROFIT

The bottom line is at the top of everyone's mind these days as America's health care system becomes increasingly profit driven. On one hand, you have the nonprofits—known for a commitment to community health care and for "doing good," using their profits to provide a service. On the other, you have for-profits—entrepreneurial-minded companies known for "doing well," using their services to gain a profit.

There are major contrasts between the two systems. One notable difference is that the for-profits are much more competitive and often promote themselves aggressively in lavish marketing campaigns, which critics say take money away from patient care. In addition, the for-profits, like any corporate entity, tend to pay their senior executives lavishly—again, too lavishly, according to critics who would rather see the money spent on more health services for members.

IT ALWAYS PAYS TO ADVERTISE

Images on TV screens and in colorful print ads tell a story of carefree, happy families, illnesses that magically disappear with the help of a compassionate doctor, with nary a bill in sight. In the real world of sickness, you probably know there's something wrong with this picture.

Yet people do, in fact, respond to those ads featuring Gene Kelly in *Singin' in the Rain,* as well as to posters in public transportation, on highway billboards, and in an endless array of magazines. How much does this advertising by the for-profit HMOs cost? The organizations that spend the marketing dollars try to keep mum on this subject. For the curious (and those with a lot of time, because tracing down such information can be tedious and time-consuming), information on for-profit versus nonprofit status as well as figures representing marketing and other administrative costs are available through the state insurance departments, which require a financial statement from all HMOs operating in the state at year's end.

MARKETING OUTLAY

In New York State, where several for-profit HMOs vie for customers, a survey by the Public Advocate for the City of New York calculated marketing expenses as percentage of hospital inpatient expenses. Here's the tally, which shows some surprising marketing outlays by nonprofit HMOs.

HMO	Status	% of hospital inpatient cost spent for marketing
Aetna Health Plans of New York	for-profit	0.8%
CIGNA	for-profit	26.9%
Empire HealthNet	nonprofit	25.0%
Health Insurance Plan of Greater N.Y.	nonprofit	3.5%
Managed Health	nonprofit	13.4%

MetLife/MetraHealth	for-profit	13.2%
Sanus	for-profit	30.1%
Travelers	for-profit	5.9%
U.S. Healthcare	for-profit	16.5%

RICH REWARDS

Like other successful companies, managed care organizations reward their executives with increases in compensation when the company does well. That's why Jeffrey M. Folick, executive vice president and chief operating officer at PacifiCare Health Systems, earned a total compensation of $10.7 million in 1995, an increase of 212 percent from the year before. Additionally, Mr. Folick received the highest stock option grant among managed care executives that year, valued at $9.8 million.

While such a funneling of funds may be good for Mr. Folick and his peers in other managed care organizations around the country, it's less than good for subscribers to the same managed care organizations, especially those subscribers who are denied coverage for potentially life-saving diagnoses and treatments.

Sometimes the executives will take the heat for poor performance. That's what happened in the case of Leonard Abramson, chairman of U.S. Healthcare, whose package for 1995 was only $2.9 million, down 23 percent from 1994. Mr. Abramson deferred more than half of his bonus until earnings per share got above $2.70 for four consecutive quarters. U.S. Healthcare was acquired by Aetna Life & Casualty in the summer of 1996 for $8.9 billion. Mr. Abramson was paid the remainder of his bonus when the deal was completed. In addition, he became fully vested in the spring of that year for stock option grants that he had deferred in 1995.

Executive pay packages aim to connect pay with the company's financial performance through the use of stock options and bonuses. Stock options aim to provide senior managers with long-term incentives for increasing shareholder value.

Bonuses at the leading managed care organizations are rewards for meeting goals such as increases in membership, revenue, and earnings or reducing operating expenses. Other compensation can include one or more of the following: premiums paid for life insurance, contributions to pension and 401K programs, deferred compensation programs, and perks, including company-sponsored transportation and travel. Needless to say, all executives receive good health care coverage.

Considering all those factors, here are some managed care executives whose 1995 compensations stood out.

Highest Compensation: $10.7 million. Jeffrey M. Folick, executive vice president and chief operating officer of PacifiCare Health Systems.

Largest Bonus: $875,000. William W. McGuire, chairman, president, and chief executive officer of United Health Care Corp.

Highest-Valued Stock Option: $9.8 million. Jeffrey M. Folick, executive vice president and chief operating officer of PacifiCare Health Systems.

Highest Salary: $1.8 million. Leonard Abramson, chairman, U.S. Healthcare, Inc.

Highest-Paid Woman: $1.9 million. Karen A. Coughlin, senior vice president, Region II, Humana, Inc.

THE INCOME ISSUE

Columnist Erma Bombeck once told her readers that the biggest lie ever foisted on the American consumer was the claim "One size fits all!" It doesn't work for hosiery, and it doesn't work for health care. Nonetheless, managed care plans across the country have developed a system in which doctors are paid a small fixed sum—generally $100 to $300 per year—that covers office care for each enrolled patient. Called *capitation*, this new payment system—rare when managed care first established their footholds in regions across the country—has become the predominant method of payment to physicians. Neither doctors nor patients are happy with this payment method. Doctors—who see their income base dwindling—contend that it's just not possible to provide endless medical care for patients when they get a return of only $300 or so a year. Patients readily understand the logic of the argument and consider the system a potential threat to their own health care.

Up to now, physicians have been paid in one or more of the following four ways.

Fee-for-Service
Fee-for-service is based on a number of set fees for certain services that are established by an individual doctor or group of

doctors. Such fees are rarely standardized but, rather, are based on such factors as the doctors' reputation, the hospital affiliation, and whether the care you need is readily available in the area.

Fee-for-service encourages doctors to use as many diagnostic tests and treatments as possible and to make as many referrals as possible. In large part, this profit incentive has contributed to this country's $4-billion annual health care bill that ultimately led to the current onslaught of managed care.

Annual Salary
Annual salary is based on a number of competitive factors, such as the number of patients the doctor cares for, how well the doctor follows standards of quality care, and how satisfied the patients are.

Annual salary may appear to be free of incentives, but in fact, this kind of payment can lead to disincentives for the doctor to establish a good patient relationship or to maintain a courteous and efficient office staff.

Capitation
Capitation, or capitated payment, is based on an arbitrary fixed amount for each patient, which is decided upon by the managed care plan and collected by the doctor whether or not care was provided to the patient.

Capitation creates an incentive for the doctor to hold down office visits, reduce the number of diagnostic tests, limit the number of referrals to specialists, and deny hospital admissions whenever possible.

Withhold Funds
A withhold fund, sometimes called a specialist fund or referral fund, involves a certain portion of a doctor's customary fee being held back until the end of the year when the sum of all the doctor's withholds is used to pay for referrals to specialists

by any of the group's doctors. After this dispersement, the remaining "kitty" is distributed to all doctors in the plan.

Withhold funds create a strong incentive to limit specialist referrals, as the fund's annual surplus is directly related to a low specialist utilization. The disinclination to refer to specialists is even stronger when each doctor's payback from the surplus fund depends on his or her own patient's use of specialists rather than on the whole group's specialist utilization.

CUTTING INTO CARE

With capitation as the front-runner in payment methods, patient advocates have been quick to side with doctors in denouncing it. If you're sick, the critics say, you are a financial liability to your doctor. Why? In order to thrive financially, your doctor needs to divide patients into two groups: Large volumes of healthy patients, who come to the office needing a minimum of financial outlay, and the other group of patients, who may, in fact, be sick and need care but don't visit the doctor to get it.

By adhering to this formula, the doctor collects a regular monthly payment without actually having to spend anything in the management of your care. Therefore, say the critics, doctors who sign up with plans that pay by capitation are prepared to sell you out in order to gain their rewards. Proponents of capitation—primarily the large HMO plans that use this method of payment—disagree.

The practice of withholding isn't the answer, either. In the trade, the usual term for this practice is *risk sharing*. In other words, if you require a lot of medical attention, you are a high risk to the doctors' income. Studies show that the higher a physician's pecuniary risk and the more that HMOs tie physician bonuses or penalties to the treatment of each individual patient, the greater the threat to the quality of care. As one doctor in an HMO with such a "risk" system wrote: "Under the risk payment HMO system, very sick patients devastate my account. Patients who come in often for care begin to look like abusers. . . . The economic incentives are clear: keep the patient away from consultants, out of the hospital, out of the office."

In the days of fee-for-service payments to doctors, many of them found an opportunity for huge payments in a practice called *fee splitting.* Very simply, this meant that a doctor who referred a patient to a specialist might be able to "share" in that specialist's fee. Doctors also began to invest in laboratories and in diagnostic facilities such as radiology centers. This led to an overuse of more expensive and less appropriate workups, which meant, in the long run, higher profits to doctors.

Proponents of the managed care system like to say that risk sharing is the inverse of fee-for-service. The truth is that risk sharing is the inverse of fee splitting. Just as fee splitting allowed doctors paid on a fee-for-service basis to profit from referring patients, so doctors under the new arrangements can profit from not referring patients.

FIVE STEPS TO PROTECT HEALTH SERVICES

As the balance continues to tilt toward the financial bottom line at the expense of medical services, it is up to each health care consumer to step up and support legislation that promotes consumer protection both on a federal and state level. Here are five ways you can help.

1. Join and/or support a grass roots advocacy group that brings these issues to light and lobbies for legislation that protects the consumer.
2. Ask your present physicians if there are any financial relationships they have with your insurance company that have the potential to create a conflict of interest and thereby compromise your care.
3. If you suspect such a situation, discourage your primary care physician from participating with these plans or get another physician.

4. Talk to your employer benefits department to express your concerns. There are many insurance companies out there for an employer to choose from.
5. Call your state agency that oversees HMOs (the complete listing is in Appendix A) and find out if complaints have been filed against any HMOs in your region that involve denial of care.

SEVEN

IS THE DOCTOR REALLY IN?

When you join an HMO, you receive a big package of promotional material, including a manual with listings of primary care doctors categorized by region and specialty. If you want to take a look at the listing before joining, call the HMOs you are interested in and ask to be connected to member services. Explain that you may join the HMO and would like to see their introductory package to make an informed choice. The office will probably not send the entire package, but you may receive a list of participating doctors.

IS YOUR DOCTOR ON THE LIST?

As you pore over the listing and look for your present doctors, you may wonder, "Is it possible for an HMO to have so many physicians service their members?" In many cases, the answer is no, or at least not each individual member. The contract struck between your employer and the HMO may include access to only a handful of the HMO's doctors, not the complete list. Understandably, an HMO is reluctant to announce this restriction prior to signing up a company's employees. Being limited to doctors in the area where you live is not necessarily a bad provision, since many studies have found that people tend to make the most use of doctors who are closest to home. The listing may also be misleading because it may be out of date: listed doctors may have retired from medical practice or no longer work for the HMO.

Far and away the most common reason that the doctor whose name appears in black and white on the list may not be available to you is that he or she may have been dropped by the HMO. Most of the time this is a cost-cutting measure. When an HMO enters a region and starts marketing its plan, it generally signs up every doctor possible. After it has established a foothold, it may begin to whittle away at the list. According to a study done for the Physician Payment Review Commission, the average yearly turnover rate for HMO doctors is 4 percent, but more than one in 10 of the plans has a turnover rate of more than 10 percent. Proponents of this practice—mostly HMOs—call this process "plan-initiated turnover" or "delisting," and they defend it as a necessary measure to keep quality high in the plans. Critics of the practice call it "economic credentialing," and they condemn it as an effort to eliminate those doctors who cost the company more in claims than their peers.

There's no way around this dilemma except to ask, outright, if the doctor you have chosen to be your primary care physician is really "on board." Don't accept "I think so," "Well, his name is there," or anything else other than a yes or no.

HOW TO GET YOUR DOCTOR ON THE LIST

If your doctor is not among those on the provider list, you have two options: Switch doctors or ask your HMO to include your doctor. While choosing a new doctor is the simplest route to continuing health care, many patients would rather fight than switch. Here are some steps that might speed the process:

1. Talk to your doctor to find out if he or she would actually want to join—or may have at one time belonged to—your HMO.

2. Write a letter to your HMO, directed to the customer relations manager, and request that your doctor be included on their list of participating doctors. Include relevant information about your doctor, including name, address, type of practice, board certification, hospital affiliations, medical society membership, and any outstanding awards or citations the doctor has received.

3. Follow up with a telephone call to the customer relations manager after a week or ten days and once again review the reasons why you think your doctor should be included in the HMO's list of participating doctors.

PART III

WHAT YOU SHOULD DO TO GET THE MOST FROM YOUR HMO

EIGHT

THE DOCTOR CHECKUP

The first task at hand for those who join an HMO or managed care plan is to choose a primary care doctor.

Your choice will be made from one of four specialists:

• *Internist:* This doctor treats adults, is trained in internal medicine, and may hold a subspecialty in cardiology, for example, or endocrinology.

• *Family practitioner:* This doctor treats adults and children and is trained in family practice.

• *Pediatrician:* This doctor treats infants and children and is trained in pediatrics.

• *Obstetrician-gynecologist:* This doctor treats adult and adolescent females and is trained in obstetrics and gynecology. Ob-gyns are accepted in many HMO networks as a primary care doctor.

PRIMARY CARE: GETTING DOWN TO BASICS

Your primary care doctor really is the one who sees you through sickness and health. In doing so, the doctor plays several different roles:

• *Caregiver.* In this role, the primary care doctor is your personal doctor and provides the medical attention you need, whether you are ready for your annual checkup or have a problem. Once a relationship has been established, this doctor may be able to answer some of your questions, and even prescribe treatment, over the telephone.

• *Gatekeeper.* Although use of this term has been vastly minimized by HMOs, the fact remains that the primary care doctor is the one who approves and authorizes referrals to specialists, hospitals, and any other medical source outside the HMO network.

• *Educator.* Whatever decisions are to be made that affect your present and long-term health should be made by you and your primary care doctor together. However, your doctor is the one with the necessary knowledge and experience to enhance and support your role in the decision-making process.

It's a big job. There are hundreds of doctors in the listings provided by your HMO who are qualified to carry it through. One hitch: The doctor who is ideal for one person may be altogether wrong for another. You can base your choice on the following four criteria.

First Criterion: Your Medical Needs

What *are* your needs? You should consider your age, sex, medical risk factors, and medical history.

If you are in general good health and don't foresee any major medical problems arising in the future, probably a doctor who is trained in one of the key primary care specialties will be able to provide appropriate care.

If you have a family history of any major disease, such as heart disease or diabetes, you should look for a primary care doctor who has a subspecialty in that field.

If indeed the possibility of a serious disease stands in your future, you must also consider which hospitals closest to you can provide the best care. If you have heart disease, the proximity of a fine cardiovascular care division won't be very helpful if your doctor is not affiliated with the institution. If you know of a hospital that you would want to be in if a worst-case scenario happens, call the institution and request a list of affiliated doctors as well as those who have admitting privileges.

Second Criterion: The Doctor's Credentials

Doctors who are affiliated with a first-rate hospital have already been screened, so you can be sure they meet the hospital's standards. But since nothing should be taken for granted when it comes to your health, you should make sure that any chosen doctor meets your standards as well.

The main credential you should be looking for is board certification. This means that a doctor has taken at least two to six years of post-medical-school training and has passed the required exam. You can find out if a doctor is board-certified by calling the American Board of Medical Specialties, at (708) 491-9091. The four specialties mentioned above are the only ones you need to be concerned about right now. Information about these and twenty-one other specialties can be found on page 129, in Appendix E, Medical Specialty Boards.

Experience is an added plus but not if it is only measured in years. An older doctor with many years of practice who is accustomed to a particular form of treatment and is unwilling to consider newer techniques may not, in fact, measure up to a younger doctor who is open to medical advances.

Note: If the doctor you are considering has been in practice for a decade or more, find out whether he or she has obtained recertification. Seventeen of the twenty-four medical specialty boards now periodically recertify their members. Again, to find out if your doctor has been recertified or if recertification is required by the particular board, call ABMS.

Another note: Most people don't think about malpractice or disciplinary actions, but you should try to find out if the doctor you are considering has been involved with any. What you want to know is whether the doctor has made an obvious error in medical care or if there is a pattern of multiple errors. You might also look for records of disciplinary actions for physical or sexual abuse of patients or for problems with drugs, alcohol, or fraud. These kinds of citations are all on record in the state agency that keeps doctors' records on file and up-to-date. They are listed in Appendix B, pages 112–117.

You can also check names in the book *10,289 Questionable Doctors*, published by the Public Citizens' Health Research Group, a consumer advocacy group based in Washington, D.C., that has been highly critical of the methods used by state medical boards to monitor their members. Public Citizen wants access to the National Practitioner Data Bank, which was created in 1986 by an act of Congress and includes names of doctors who have lost their license, lost clinical privileges, and even been targeted by professional societies. The Data Bank contains the names of over 62,000 health care providers with disciplinary problems—licensing action, malpractice judgments, or settlements.

To find out more about the National Practitioner Data Bank, which is located in Rockville, Maryland, call (301) 443-2300.

Third Criterion: The Doctor's Practice
The best doctor is not much good to you if you don't have access to care when you need it. Ideally, your primary care doctor will be located near where you live or where you work. This makes sense for emergencies when you need attention fast; it also makes sense for preventive care, which you are more apt to take advantage of if it's close by. There are a number of key questions to ask about a doctor's practice, and many of them can be answered by the doctor's assistant or office manager.

1. How long does it take to get an appointment for a routine examination or nonurgent medical condition?
2. How long will it take to be seen by the primary care doctor in case of an emergency?
3. What is the doctor's backup system for covering emergencies when the office is not open?
4. What is the doctor's policy for referrals to specialists?

5. Can you choose a specialist out of the HMO network and still be referred by your doctor?
6. Does the office have billing procedures for regular copayments, or must payment be made at the time of the visit?
7. Does the office send out reminder notices for appointments?
8. How much time does the doctor generally allot for a routine physical examination?
9. Does the doctor use a private laboratory for blood testing?
10. Does the doctor perform medical tests such as EKG or stress testing in the office?

Be sure to take notes in the course of the conversation with the doctor's office and note the name of the person you speak to. You can then present the information in black and white if it doesn't happen the way you were led to believe it would.

REFERRALS VERSUS SECOND OPINIONS

There are two reasons why your primary care doctor would recommend that you consult with another doctor: One, with the expectation that the second doctor can improve upon the treatment already underway, and two, with the expectation that the second doctor will confirm the appropriateness of that treatment.

- *Referral.* It would be impossible for a primary care physician—even the best—to know everything there is to know about every medical condition. That's where specialists come in, and the ease with which this entry is achieved can have a considerable impact on your recovery. If you have a skin condition that isn't responding to treatment or an allergy that seems to be getting worse, you need the expertise and experience of a physician whose practice is limited to, in these particular cases, dermatology or allergy/immunology. In a managed care environment, doctors are often reluctant to refer patients to specialists as frequently as they might have in the "old days" since the HMO may frown upon the high cost of medical care involved in specialty care. If you feel that the current treatment offered by your primary care doctor is not working as well as it should, ask your doctor to refer you to a specialist. If your doctor hesitates or refuses outright, you may need to find a specialist on your-own and pay for whatever portion of the fee is not covered by your HMO (which may be all of it). If you do seek a specialist's care and your HMO denies payment for the treatment, you should follow through with a forceful but firm letter giving the specifics of why you believe the treatment is essential. (Need help with that letter? See Chapter 13.)

· *Second Opinion.* Your primary care doctor may want confirmation that the proposed treatment is appropriate. Let's say your doctor has concluded that your back pain is almost certainly the result of kidney stones and that you should undergo a procedure called lithotripsy to break up the stones. Here's where a second opinion from a urologist is advisable, either to confirm that the procedure is the best choice or to recommend another, perhaps less drastic choice of treatment. Most HMOs are happy to pay for second opinions because the new consultation may result in less care at a lower cost.

Fourth Criterion: The Doctor's Manner

We're talking personality here, and if yours and the doctor's don't click, it will be very difficult for you to get the best medical care. Even when you've done everything possible to choose the best doctor and select someone you feel is going to deliver superior care, you may walk into the doctor's office and feel that you've made a mistake. While your inclination in the face of such an event might be to leave immediately, don't, for two reasons. One, a certain amount of time has already been set aside for your consultation, and if you were to leave, both the doctor and the office staff would have justification for annoyance. Second, and more important, your first negative impression may be overridden by a pleasant and informative consultation. Certainly you want to give yourself every advantage in finding Dr. Right.

Sometimes bad chemistry has to do with a doctor's personal style, such as a gruff, authoritarian manner. It may even have to do with how the furniture is arranged in the office, such as a chair that is so far from the doctor's desk that you must lean forward to partake in a conversation. In more cases than are necessary, a first encounter with a new primary care doctor is in the examination room, where it is natural to feel anxious. But you can make the situation easier by initiating conversation and giving the doctor a chance to respond to your comments about pictures on the wall, your trip to the office, or even the fact that you are very nervous.

People often have trouble talking to their doctor because they really want to know the answers to questions that are difficult to ask. Here are some questions that can help give an idea of how receptive a doctor is to answering questions.

Ten Questions to Get the Conversation Going
1. What tests will be done and what is the reason for each one?
2. Are there any alternatives to the recommended medical tests?
3. If you need a prescription, will the doctor order a generic version?
4. If you need a new medication, will the doctor give you some free samples?
5. Will the doctor explain the possible side effects of your prescription?
6. If the diagnosis is serious and scary, can you get a second opinion?

7. Will the doctor use any X rays you've had taken within the past month?
8. Will the doctor give you an itemized bill?
9. Will the doctor give you approximate times you can telephone the office if necessary?
10. Will the doctor negotiate fees?

NINE

RETAIN YOUR RIGHTS

How can you help your doctor be a better doctor? The answer: by being a better patient. It is true that medical care is a collaborative effort between you and your physician. You can only assume your share of responsibility in the physician-patient relationship when you are sure that your fundamental needs are met. Know that you have certain individual and inalienable rights as a patient. The American Medical Association put forth a "bill of rights" in 1989 called "Fundamental Elements of the Patient-Physician Relationship." If you want further information about this report, contact the American Medical Association (AMA) at (312) 464-5000.

The report makes several important assertions:

You—the patient—have the right to make decisions regarding your medical treatment. You are free to accept or refuse health care that is recommended by your doctor. Your right to refuse treatment has been established in a series of landmark cases; nothing may be done to you without your informed consent. The freedom to refuse health care includes the freedom to decline all life-prolonging medical treatments including medication and artificially or technologically supplied respiration, nutrition, or hydration. Even in a hospital, you have the right to say no to excessive probing and pricking of your body. Few have the courage to stand up for this right, but as a patient, you can wield power.

You—the patient—have the right to expect courtesy, respect, dignity, responsiveness, and timely attention to your needs. Everyone knows what it is like to have to undress and wait endlessly in a cold examining room. You actually have the right to get dressed and walk out, if not onto the street, at least to the staff area, where you can insist that you be seen promptly.

You—the patient—have the right to confidentiality. The doctor must keep your communications confidential unless you have expressly and in writing given consent otherwise.

THE MENTAL HEALTH DILEMMA

Nowhere is the issue of confidentiality more of a concern than in the case of mental health treatment. Mental health care providers contend that rules imposed by HMOs and other managed care organizations produce a powerful incentive to undertreat or deny treatment altogether. But there is good news. In 1996 President Clinton signed into law a national bill that requires employers with fifty or more employees to improve health care coverage for workers with mental illnesses. The bill, included as part of the 1997 Veterans Affairs, Housing and Urban Development, and Independent Agencies Appropriations, will go into effect in January 1998. Laws in many individual states already require that health care plans incorporate treatment of mental illnesses. The new law is designed to make caps on mental illnesses equal with caps on physical illnesses. At the moment, most insurance policies include a $50,000 lifetime cap for treatment of mental illnesses, while the cap for physical illnesses might be $1 million or more. A $50,000 cap can be quickly absorbed in a short period of time just by paying for hospital stays for individuals with mental illnesses.

If your employer is aware of your ongoing treatment, you should have a talk with your benefits coordinator as soon as possible to determine what part of your treatment will be covered under the new plan. If your employer does not know of your treatment and you would prefer to keep it confidential, you may have to find a way to pay for the treatment on your own. The most obvious solution is to work out a payment plan with your therapist or to work a treatment program that will still be effective at the least possible cost.

If you believe that you are being denied mental health care, call your state HMO regulator (see Appendix A).

You—the patient—have the right to essential health care. Federal laws provide safeguards against your being turned away from a hospital emergency room when you're in need of immediate treatment, regardless of your ability to pay for it.

You—the patient—have the right to continuity of health care. If, for some reason, your doctor leaves the HMO or decides to drop you as a patient, you are still entitled to have continued care if such care is medically indicated. You must be given a reasonable amount of time to secure alternative care.

YOU CAN TAKE IT WITH YOU

The guarantee of health care coverage for persons who transfer jobs is a landmark achievement. Many working Americans find themselves in a situation of job lock—wanting to leave a job but fearful of doing so because it might mean loss of health benefits. As many as three out of ten Americans have at some time made a decision to stay in a job they hate simply because loss of medical coverage could be too costly to justify the change.

Job-locked individuals report a wide range of concerns: Employees who enjoy coverage for dental and eye care and for psychiatric counseling are justifiably concerned that a new job might not have these "extras." Given the rapidity with which health care companies change and even disappear, some workers become concerned that a new job might not offer any benefits at all. Many are reluctant to leave a job where they were covered for treatment of an illness that, in a new job, would be considered a pre-existing condition.

Many of these concerns were effectively eliminated with the passage of a new law, called the Health Insurance Portability and Accountability Act of 1996, that protects people from losing their health coverage as a result of a job change. The concept of *portability* means that anyone who is insured by an employer is entitled to sign up for whatever health insurance a new employer offers without a waiting period. This guarantees access to health care without disruption for those moving to a company that offers benefits; however, it does not guarantee health care benefits if the new company does not offer any plan. It also does not allow for a more generous package in a new job unless that type of coverage is the only choice offered by the new employer.

If you are planning to move into a new job with a different employer, how do you find out about the kind of health care coverage you can expect? Make sure you have a complete and current benefits package at your present place of employment. This will provide all the necessary information about your current coverage. If possible, get a complete and current benefits package from the benefits office manager at your new place of work. You will have to study the two carefully to determine the similarities and differences. What's more, you will have to decide if and how you will be able to handle any health care costs that might not be covered by your new employer.

Another possible solution: If you find that your old health care coverage is markedly superior to what you are heading for, consider discussing the situation with the benefits manager. If the costs are within the same range, your new employer might decide to switch health plans or add another choice for all employees.

Here are some typical cases affected by the new law:

- *A female office worker is diagnosed with breast cancer and undergoes chemotherapy, which is paid for by her employer's health care plan. Her disease goes into remission for five years and she is considered disease free. She is offered a job with a new company, but she is concerned that any future cancer treatment will not be covered under the new health plan.* This woman can change jobs and still be entitled to health coverage with the new employer no matter what illness she is being treated for and with no limitations on treatment of her preexisting condition.

- *A salesman works for a company whose health care plan covers his son, who undergoes monthly treatments for asthma. He would like to accept a new job but does not want to lose health care benefits for his child.* The law provides a guarantee of continuation of coverage with a new company for the man's dependent child if the new company offers a health care plan. The company cannot deny coverage for the child on the basis of a preexisting condition.

- *A sixty-year-old man wants to take an early retirement because of a heart problem. He is not old enough to qualify for Medicare and is worried that he will not be able to get insurance coverage.* Any insurance company that offers individual coverage must write a policy for this individual. However, there are no parameters included in the law about the cost of the coverage, which the insurance company may set at any level they choose.

- *As a result of a divorce, a woman loses the health care coverage provided under the policy offered by her husband's employer.*

She is willing to purchase her own health care policy, but because of a preexisting diabetes condition, she cannot find a company to insure her. Any insurance company that offers individual insurance must write a policy for this woman, although they are only restricted by existing state requirements in the rates they set for this insurance. Consequently, even though she may now be covered, the cost of this coverage may be too high.

You—the patient—have the right to receive information. You are entitled to know the benefits, risks, and costs of the treatment alternatives that are appropriate for your condition. You should receive guidance from your doctor as to the optimal course of action, have your questions answered, and receive a second, independent opinion. What this comes down to is that you have the right to ask questions. It's your most important right, and you should exercise it often.

"GAG" CLAUSES ARE NO JOKE

Advertisements for HMOs often include a reassuring picture of a doctor and patient in close conversation. But such images belie a hidden truth behind the contracts that bind doctors to HMOs: These contracts may include *gag clauses*, provisions that limit the doctors from talking freely with patients about costly treatment options or HMO payment policies, including the financial incentives for doctors to withhold care.

When doctors across the country first began to complain about these restrictions on the way they practiced medicine, such complaints were assumed to be simply cries of anguish from a group of high-money earners who were worried about dwindling income. But then some actual contracts came to light, and in the media frenzy that followed, top executives at many of the nation's leading HMOs found themselves in an uncomfortably hot spotlight.

U.S. Healthcare's original gag clause, which became the subject of media attention, reads: "Physicians shall agree not to take any action or make any communication which undermines or could undermine the confidence of enrollees, potential enrollees, their employers, their unions, or the public in U.S. Healthcare or the quality of U.S. Healthcare coverage. Physicians shall keep the Proprietary Information (payment rates, utilization review procedures, etc.) and this Agreement strictly confidential."

Once the silence was broken, physicians from other HMOs came forward to report similar clauses in contracts with other HMOs. When the smoke had cleared, U.S. Healthcare's offending clause had undergone a revision: "(1) Physician shall have the right and is encouraged to discuss with his or her patients pertinent details regarding the diagnosis of the patient's condition, the nature and purpose of any recommended procedure, the potential risks and benefits of any recommended treatment, and any reasonable alternatives to such recommended treatment. (2) Physician's obligations not to disclose Proprietary Information do not apply to any disclosures to a patient determined by Physician to be necessary or appropriate for the diagnosis and care of a patient except to the extent such disclosure would otherwise violate Physician's legal or ethical obligations. (3) Physician is encouraged to discuss U.S. Healthcare's provider reimbursement methodology with Physician's patients, subject only to Physician's general contractual and ethical obligations not to make false or misleading statements. Accordingly, Proprietary Information does not include descriptions of the Quality Care Compensation System methodology under which Physician is reimbursed, although such information does include the specific rates paid by U.S. Healthcare due to their competitively sensitive nature."

State lawmakers wasted little time in responding to the demands of doctors and patient advocates for reform. The swift bipartisan response demonstrates the volatile climate in which HMOs and insurance companies now operate. States adopting laws to combat gag clauses include California, Colorado, Delaware, Georgia, Indiana, Maine, Maryland, Massachusetts, New Hampshire, New York, Pennsylvania, Rhode Island, Tennessee, Vermont, Virginia, and Washington. Each state law is a little different, but at very least they protect the right of doctors and patients to discuss all treatment options.

Is there such a law in your state, and if so, what does it say? To find out, call the state agency that licenses HMOs. These agencies are listed in Appendix A, pages 103–111.

If you think your doctor is withholding information about treatment, what should you do? The first step should be to ask the doctor directly if the suggested treatment or choice of treatments are the only options for your condition. For instance, if you have been diagnosed with rheumatoid arthritis and the doctor has recommended your taking steroids, you might ask if a newer drug—a very low dose chemotherapy drug—might not be effective. You could also ask if acupuncture might be helpful in your case. Such an inquiry should not be confrontational, and by all means, you should be armed with some good solid literature to back you up, not just hearsay.

If your doctor remains adamant about the course of your treatment and you still suspect that better alternatives are available, write a letter to the state agency and present a brief summary of the particular episode with your doctor. Include in the letter the name and address of the HMO you belong to and the full name and specialty of the doctor. Send a copy of the letter to the HMO's office.

You—the patient—have a right to see your medical records. Trying to examine your medical or hospital records used to be nearly impossible. Doctors and hospitals have traditionally held that all records are their exclusive property and have not, as a rule, been willing to release them to patients. Times have changed; today almost every state allows some form of access to records, ranging from the right to inspect to the right to copy. In states with laws in place, the regulators for hospitals, doctors, and HMOs can brief you on the procedures for getting your records. In Appendices A, B, and C you will find the appropriate place to call or write. In states without a law in place, patient-access policies can vary from hospital to hospital and doctor to doctor. Basically, though, there are certain general points to keep in mind:

• Most state laws require a written request. Many hospitals have a standard "release of information" authorization form that you can ask for. To get your records from your doctor, write a letter requesting the records and include the following information: date and purpose of the request, reports required, specific treatment dates, your address and signature. It is not usually necessary to have the request notarized.

• Call the doctor's office or hospital to find out if there are any charges to get the records. Don't be surprised to find up to a $1 per page charge for copies of records, and even higher if the records are stored in microfilm. Extra charges may include processing fees and postage. If the state law does not specify fees, a hospital may set its own. You might have the option of reviewing the records first, however, which will enable you to pick and choose which pages or sets of records you really want, rather than ordering an entire set.

• If you find a glaring error in your records, contact the doctor's office or the director of the hospital's medical record department to report it. Follow through to make sure the error is corrected, and find out if the records have been forwarded to any other doctor or agency. Insist that the records be corrected in each instance.

• There is no time limit on requesting your records. However, be aware that the records are available for only as long as the doctor or hospital keeps them. Some facilities retain records indefinitely, while others keep them for only a limited number of years.

• To find out about the laws in your state, contact your state hospital association, your state legislator, or the American Medical Record Association, Director of Public Relations, 919 North Michigan Avenue, Suite 1400, Chicago, IL 60611.

PROTECT
YOUR PRIVACY

Not long ago, medical records were secure in filing cabinets, locked away in a doctor's office. Today they're probably included in a computer file, available on-line, owned by partnerships and provider networks, and accessible by computer hackers, lawyers, and others who have little to do with medical treatment. Furthermore, under managed care's new economics based on capitated contracts with doctors, patient records are frequently scrutinized—again by individuals who have nothing to do with actual medical care—for "missteps" in what the plan considers to be necessary cost effectiveness.

These changes mean that medical records are now commercial commodities, used for claims reviews, compliance surveys, and credentialing decisions as well as for marketing purposes and who knows what else. The procedure for obtaining medical and hospital records is presented in the previous chapter on page 59.

Managed care companies may create other problems for patients who justifiably assume that their medical information is private. These companies may market that information to pharmaceutical companies and other commercial outlets. This defies the physician-patient relationship, according to the code of the American Medical Association, because it violates principles of informed consent and patient confidentiality. And because the AMA's code sets forth de facto legal obligations, this practice may expose the physician to a lawsuit. You can find out if your doctor has been involved in such a lawsuit (or in any lawsuit, for that matter) in the aforementioned *10,289 Questionable Doctors*, a two-volume book published by Public Citizen in Washington, D.C. ([202] 588-7780). If you have access to the on-line service LEXIS-NEXIS, you can run a search of the doctor's background or can have the search run by the service for a charge of $.05 per line, with a $6 minimum. To contact LEXIS-NEXIS, call (800) 346-9759.

Though these managed care contracts are risky, the danger they may pose pales in comparison to that of computerized information systems that give network physicians immediate access to a patient's latest medical history. The vastness of such information systems makes it simple for strangers to copy records, leaving little or no trace, especially if the files are on-line. Invisible alteration of patient records is also much simpler, and only when a patient insists on a correction—sometimes with the threat of a lawsuit—may the error be detected.

The AMA has promulgated a laundry list of computerized medical record protection guidelines. Chief among them is informing the patient of the existence of the computerized database, the persons or companies who have access to the patient's computer files, and the nature of the access. Security systems also should be installed. The AMA recommends "passwords, encryption (encoding) of information, and scannable badges or other user identification." Finally, computer access should be limited to authorized persons, and while the AMA doesn't suggest it, employees and persons with access to the database should sign a confidentiality agreement.

As managed care continues to challenge the physician-patient relationship, patient privacy's grip will doubtless tighten in response, creating greater burdens for physicians.

Many states, spurred in part to shield the identity of persons with HIV and other communicable diseases, have enacted expansive privacy laws and patient "bills of rights" that, if violated, could result in civil liability, medical license revocation, or even criminal conviction. Privacy statutes have been sharpened over time. There's no single guide to patient privacy, but there are some basic patient-privacy principles everyone should know.

WHAT THE LAW SAYS

Some forty states and the District of Columbia formally recognize a physician-patient privilege. While the scope of the privilege varies, it generally prohibits a physician from testifying about any patient matter learned by the doctor in the course of the physician-patient relationship unless otherwise required by law. In some states the patient's very identity is privileged. Some states require a court order, not just a subpoena, for a physician to testify about a patient's medical information, and a doctor who responds to only a subpoena may be sued by the patient. Still other states treat physicians as trustees and will allow patients to sue if the trust is violated. If you want to know where your own state stands on these issues, contact the American Health Information Management Association (AHIMA), 919 North Michigan Avenue, Suite 1400, Chicago, IL 60611, attention Professional Practice Division, or call (312) 787-2672.

KEEPING IT PRIVATE

- Find out about your company's policies before you get sick. If you're seriously ill, you may not be thinking clearly enough to check out your rights.

- Become familiar with the Americans with Disabilities Act. It's meant to prevent discrimination based on disability, but it protects nondisabled workers as well. Call the Job Accommodation Network at (800) ADA-WORK.
- Check with your state's labor department to learn if your state also has laws protecting your rights. A few states have laws that provide even greater protection than the ADA.
- If your company is self-insured, check with your personnel or benefits department for its confidentiality policy on handling health insurance claims. Ask who has access.
- Modify blanket medical release forms that allow employers or insurers access to all of your records. Write in exactly what information can or cannot be released; for instance, only information related to specific illness or injury.

BIG BROTHER WITH A ZILLION BYTES

The transgressions of individual doctors in letting private patient information slip away pale in comparison to the way medical records are funneled to the Medical Information Bureau. The MIB, a nonprofit organization run by about 700 life insurers, maintains medical records on about 15 million people. The MIB compiles coded reports on blood pressure, cholesterol, and other health risk factors such as sexual practices, driving records, and leisure activities, including risky activities such as hang-gliding or mountain climbing. The reports are used by insurance companies to identify high-risk individuals and fraudulent insurance applications.

The MIB has far-reaching implications for patients. The biggest problem is that the information on the records is not always accurate; in fact, some 450,000 to 600,000 of the files on the MIB system reportedly contain significant errors. If yours is one of them, the MIB might falsely identify you as having cancer or Alzheimer's disease or AIDS.

To keep your medical records private or at least restrict them to those who need the data for a legitimate reason, you should bring up the subject of confidentiality during your first meeting with a doctor.

THE ANATOMY OF A CONSENT

When it comes to the privacy of medical records, there is no perfect protection. But if your physician wants to submit your medical records to anyone—an insurance company, a lawyer, another doctor—you should request a consent form. Here's what such a form should include:

- Name of the doctor or other health care provider releasing the information
- Name and address of the company or individual requesting the information
- Patient's name, address, and date of birth
- Purpose of the disclosure of information (for instance, an insurance dispute, second opinion, life insurance application, or malpractice case)
- Identification of the exact records being released, with precise treatment dates and illness details
- Date when the consent will expire
- Date the consent was drawn up
- Patient's signature with date signed
- Doctor's signature with date signed
- Clause prohibiting the recipient's disclosure of the information without the patient's written consent

Here is a sample consent form:

Ivan Smith, M.D.
600 Sixth Street
Smithville, NY 10000

January 2, 1998

ABC Insurance Company
4000 Fourth Street
Chicago, IL 60000

To Whom It May Concern:
This will acknowledge your request for the medical records of patient Jane Jones, who resides at 700 Seventh Street, Smithville, NY 10000; DOB 2-17-44.

As per your request, you will use this information for the specific purpose of writing a life insurance policy for Ms. Jones.

I am releasing medical records of Ms. Jones for the period that she was in my care for a broken foot. Treatment began on June 1, 1997, and concluded on August 1, 1997. You are entitled to use the attached medical information up to and including March 1, 1998. At that time, the consent will expire and I request that the medical file be returned to me at the above address.

Signed
     Ivan Smith, M.D.
Signed   _____
     Jane Jones
Date   _____

A copy of the form should be kept in your medical file, but it wouldn't be a bad idea to check on the location of that file. It should be in a secure place, with only authorized persons allowed access. If medical files are computerized, the system should contain appropriate security controls, and access passwords should be changed frequently. You should also be given a copy for your own files at home.

MORE TO DO

Don't stop with a consent form. There are a number of other steps you can take to protect your medical privacy.

Read before you sign. Before signing off on a blanket release form that allows employers and insurers access to all your medical records, look for ways to modify it. For example, insert a phrase that limits the number of doctors who are allowed to release your records or designate that records may be released only for the period of time of your hospitalization or treatment, thereby cutting off perpetual permission to get into your files. You should make certain, however, that reimbursement isn't contingent upon your signing the standard form.

Make sure your medical records are accurate. Ask your doctor for copies of your medical files. If you have trouble getting your doctor to give you your files, you can ask another doctor (a specialist you are seeing, a friend, a friend's friend) to request them; professionals usually agree to this as a professional courtesy. If that fails, get a lawyer; often a letter on legal letterhead will be persuasion enough.

Find out what the data bank knows about you. Approximately one out of every seven Americans has a personal record on file with the Medical Information Bureau (MIB). If you would like to see yours, you can request it free of charge from MIB, Box 105, Essex Station, Boston, MA 02112, or call (617) 426-3660. You will receive a form to complete, and this will begin the process. If you find errors in your records on file at MIB—and many people do—request that they be corrected. You should send a statement from your doctor with the correct information. Follow through to make sure the error has been completed.

Go "off the record" with your doctor. If you have any medical problems that are particularly sensitive, you might ask your doctor *not* to include them in your file. This is a far wiser option than not telling your doctor about certain aspects of your medical history (sexual practices, past or current use of drugs, psychological disorders, etc.) for fear of repercussions.

Know the law. The Americans with Disabilities Act (ADA), which went into effect in 1992, makes it illegal for companies to ask any questions about the disability or medical history of a job applicant. The law forbids discrimination on the basis of medical history in hirings or promotions. For more information about the law, contact the Job Accommodation Network at (800) ADA-WORK. A hot line is open Monday through Thursday, 8 A.M. to 8 P.M., and Friday, 8 A.M. to 5 P.M.

ELEVEN

WHEN THE HMO WON'T PAY

In addition to state-by-state legislation mandating the provision of certain levels of care, courts are increasingly allowing suits brought by patients who feel that care has been unjustifiably withheld to proceed against managed care organizations.

The most famous example remains *Fox* vs. *Health Net, Inc.*, a 1992 case in which a California jury awarded $77 million in punitive damages and $12 million in compensatory damages to the family of a thirty-eight-year-old mother who ultimately died from breast cancer after the HMO denied coverage for a bone marrow transplant. (Later, both parties settled for an undisclosed sum.) The HMO had maintained that the procedure was not covered because it was "experimental/investigational." The plaintiff's attorney argued that the HMO's definition of "investigational" procedures was so ambiguous that it could include virtually any medical procedure. In addition, evidence was introduced that the HMO allegedly utilized financial incentives to encourage its claims examiners to deny coverage for costly procedures.

An arbitration panel awarded $1 million in that same year against the parent company of that same California HMO for another case in which the HMO similarly denied treatment for a cancer patient on the grounds that it was "experimental/investigational." The arbitration panel found that the treatment was not experimental because it was being increasingly used in cancer cases with some clinical success, and the arbitrators found the term *investigational* to be too ambiguous to be used as a basis for denying coverage. The arbitrators furthermore found that the HMO had sought to interfere in the physician-patient relationship by pressuring the patient's physician to reverse his support for the treatment. The arbitrators concluded that the actions of the HMO constituted "extreme and outrageous behavior exceeding all bounds usually tolerated in a civilized society."

Among the top ten monetary legal decisions of 1995 was a $40-million verdict in Fulton County, Georgia, against Kaiser Permanente, the largest HMO in the country. The family of a six-month-old boy with a rare clotting disease alleged that he lost both hands and both legs following a cardiorespiratory arrest during the trip to the hospital. The HMO had directed the family to a hospital forty-two miles from his home, where the HMO received a 15 percent discount, despite the fact that the child had a 104-degree temperature. In October 1995, a Cook County, Illinois, jury awarded approximately $9.7 million on behalf of a newborn suffering mental retardation against the mother's primary care physician, a family practitioner, who acted as the HMO's "gatekeeper" for referrals to specialists. That primary care physician appropriately referred the mother to an ob-gyn upon the diagnosis of pregnancy and did not provide any other prenatal care. However, the primary care physician received, initialed, and forwarded to the obstetrician the results of blood sugar tests that revealed the mother had gestational diabetes. The obstetrician apparently failed to review those results (and settled out of court for his policy limits). The primary care physician argued that she should not be held liable for failing to review and act upon the laboratory results, because she had referred the patient to a specialist for further care. The jury, however, refused to absolve the primary care physician of continued responsibility for the overall coordination and supervision of the patient's care.

In December 1995, a Portland, Oregon, HMO decided not to take its chances with a jury and settled a member's wrongful denial of benefits claim for $1 million. In that case, *Thomas* vs. *Sisters of Providence Good Health Plan of Oregon, Inc.* (Oregon Circuit Court, Multnomah County), the plaintiff's neurosurgeon recommended surgery for a compressed nerve root, but the HMO denied the request and recommended physical therapy. The patient's primary care physician appealed that denial, and seven months later, the HMO approved the surgery. However, permanent nerve damage had occurred by that time. The clear message that the public, legislators, judges, and juries are sending is that there are boundaries to the extent to which managed care organizations can limit access to health care.

HANDLING PROBLEMS: FIRST THINGS FIRST

Before you get to the point where you have to resort to legal action to fight denial of care, there are a number of steps you can take to protect yourself even after you sign up with an HMO.

Know your benefits as they are stated on your schedule of benefits. Be absolutely clear about them, and if you're not, call the member services department of the HMO and get the information in writing. Some plans have an "opt out" clause that allows you to seek care from a non-HMO doctor if you pay all or part of the fee. Most plans contain a number of clauses, and you must understand them all.

Work with the HMO through your primary care doctor, who coordinates your treatments and refers you to specialists. If the doctor is a good advocate, your case will gain support; at the very least, you will know why a claim is being denied. If the doctor is not a good advocate, consider changing doctors.

Make sure all forms are filled out properly just as the HMO requires. If anything is wrong—a missing or improperly completed form—the HMO is likely to deny the claim or delay payment until the form is corrected. One of the advantages of being in an HMO is not having to fill out lengthy claims forms as with indemnity insurance companies. The downside of this is that your HMO doctor may inadvertently make a mistake on the form. Ask to see all forms before they are submitted to the HMO office on your behalf.

Create a paper trail by getting a second opinion on your own and having this specialist write a letter to your HMO doctor giving justification for denied treatment. If this doesn't work, send a copy of the second opinion to the HMO office yourself. At the point that you learn that a treatment has been denied, write down everything that happened in the course of your attempt to get treatment, starting from your first visit to your primary care doctor.

HANDLING PROBLEMS: DON'T GIVE UP

There are still a number of steps you can take to get the HMO to change its mind about denying your treatment.

File an immediate appeal to the HMO, and in so doing, make sure you check your HMO handbook carefully for any specific instructions you need to follow. If your handbook instructs you to direct your letter to a specific department, do so. Otherwise, send your letter to Member Services at the address for the HMO listed in your handbook. Make sure all communication is by registered mail—a security measure—even though you are not required to do so. Keep copies of your letters and keep a record of the dates of your letters and of the HMO's responses. What should the letter say? Turn to Chapter 13, page 76, for an example of this type of letter and others. *Do it now:* In most cases you have sixty days from the date of the denial form in which to file your letter of appeal. The sooner the better.

Be firm and businesslike and let the HMO know that you won't take no for an answer. Resubmit the first letter that explains why you feel you are entitled to payment for the treatment and why you feel denial is wrong. In this letter, include the following legal disclaimer: "This appeal relates only to the denial of the benefits in question, but does not constitute and shall in no way be deemed an admission that I am limited in my right to pursue a 'Bad Faith' remedy in state court." This statement suggests to the HMO that you have consulted with a lawyer on the matter and that you intend to pursue the denial into the courts, if necessary.

File a complaint with the state insurance department. This complaint will take anywhere from a month to a year to process. In the meantime, let the HMO know that you have filed this complaint and continue to send your letters asking for the HMO's action in remedying the denial of coverage.

Hire a lawyer who will advise you whether the HMO can be sued for bad faith. If so, you may be entitled to punitive or emotional distress damages as well as the benefits owed. This step applies only to those who are enrolled in an HMO as an individual or family, not to those who are part of an employer group plan.

TWELVE

KEEP YOUR OWN
REPORT CARD

"Report cards" rating HMOs on various general criteria seemed to be a good idea when they were proposed in the mid 1990s. But when surveys and rankings became a cottage industry in the media, what got lost in the shuffle was the original intent: to give consumers a solid benchmark for assessing their own HMO.

No matter. All the data one HMO or another includes in such a report card can be of great interest to employers or government policy makers but may have no relevance to consumers. What matters, after all, is not so much whether one HMO provided more immunizations than any other but whether *your* child was immunized on schedule and whether the doctor conducted the procedure with compassion and concern for the child and other family members.

What do consumers want? Information on which doctors belong to a plan, what services are covered, and how satisfied members are with the plan. The fact is that disenrollment rates would be the best check of consumer satisfaction; even then, though, what makes one member unhappy may not bother another member at all.

The answer: a report card of your own. Here's a sample structure. You can add to it as necessary to be personally helpful.

REPORT CARD

FOR: XYZ HEALTH PLAN
111 First Street
New City, NY 10000
711-777-1111

DOCTOR: James Cook, M.D.

PATIENT: Mary Smith

Scheduled routine appointment for checkup
Scheduled appointment for emergency visit
Scheduled referral to specialist
Doctor's availability during nonoffice hours
Doctor's punctuality for office visit
Doctor's personal manner
Doctor's explanation of illness and medicines
Courtesy of office staff
Office informing about test results
Overall evaluation
Rating Scale:
X=satisfactory   XX=good   XXX=very good   XXXX=excellent

THIRTEEN

PUT IT IN
WRITING

When something goes wrong in the way your HMO handles your health care coverage—whether it's denial of care, mis-scheduling of an appointment, discourteous treatment, or mis-handling of medical records, to name only a few of the possibilities—the immediate impulse is to pick up the tele-phone and spill out your anger to whoever happens to answer the call at the HMO. Letting off steam usually accomplishes very little; a better way is to put your complaint in writing.

Many people shun letter writing because they think their use of language is not effective or that their handwriting is poor. But letter writing—if it's done properly—is no more difficult than making out a shopping list, and possibly a lot more pro-ductive.

What follows are a few of the letters that you might have occasion to write in the course of your dealings with your HMO. Use them verbatim or as a pattern, and soon you may not need to use them at all.

WHAT A LETTER SHOULD SAY

Your letter should include the following points:

- What you want the HMO to do for you; that is, the action the recipient should take on your behalf;
- Why you think it's important that the HMO take the particular action you're requesting;
- Specific information that might be necessary for the HMO to act on your request. At the very least, attach copies of the original medical record (see Chapter 9, page 59, for steps to get your medical records);
- Anything you believe will encourage the recipient to take action on your behalf.

Appeal About Denial of Coverage

January 1, 1998

Family Health Coverage, Inc.
Attn.: Martha Beyers/Manager, Customer Service
200 Park Avenue South
New York, NY 10011

RE: Identification No: 300-68-3267
      Case No. 192
      Patient: Jennifer Atkins
      Dates of Service: June 1, 1997–August 1, 1997

Dear Ms. Beyers:

Your letter of December 15, 1997, denies coverage for the physical therapy treatments I received for arthritis during the above time period. According to the benefits specified in my member contract, dated May 17, 1997, certain nonmedical treatments, such as physical therapy, are covered by Family Health Coverage.

I would like to make you aware of certain points:

1. I was referred to the physical therapist by my primary care doctor, Peter Fox, M.D., who is part of Family Health Coverage.
2. Your member benefits contract clearly states that this type of therapy is covered with a $10 copay from me.
3. The treatments have helped me considerably; in fact, I have been able to reduce the dosage of pain medication that had been prescribed at the onset of the condition.

I submitted the claim to Family Health Coverage immediately after the course of therapy was completed. Several months then passed before I heard from your company and your response was a denial of my claim. The delay in responding to the claim is unacceptable. The denial of payment in light of the above stated facts is even more unacceptable. If the matter is not settled within the next 30 days, I will take my complaint to the State Commissioner of Insurance, the Better Business Bureau, and the State Attorney General.

I expect a response by return mail.

Very truly yours,

Complaint About Errors in Medical File

January 1, 1998

David Linden, M.D.
14 Broadhurst Avenue
Kingston, IL 60606

Dear Dr. Linden:

It has come to my attention that the medical files on record in your office contain a serious error. I wish to have the error corrected.

In September of 1997 I visited your office on three separate occasions for treatment of pain in my lower back. At the time, you diagnosed the problem as a muscle spasm and prescribed a muscle relaxant for the back problem. In addition, you prescribed a mild sedative because I told you that increased responsibilities at work had put me under a great deal of stress. You did not, as you have noted in my record, recommend psychological therapy, nor did I discuss the possibilities of such treatment. The medical prescriptions were quite effective and within a month the symptoms had disappeared.

Therefore, I want you to do the following:

1. Revise my medical file, removing all references to psychological therapy. Most important, destroy the file containing this reference.
2. Contact any other doctor or agency to whom my medical file may have been sent to inform them of the error and to ensure that the error has been corrected.
3. Inform me immediately, in writing, that you have received this letter and that you intend to act upon my request.
4. Acknowledge as soon as possible, in writing, that my records have been corrected and that you have contacted any other persons or agencies who might have copies of the erroneous records and have ensured that the error has been corrected.
5. Send me a copy of the corrected records.

I await your prompt reply.

Sincerely yours,

Transferring Medical Records

January 1, 1998

Jane K. Andover, M.D.
1430 West Broadway
Tempe, AZ 85282

Dear Dr. Andover,

As I told you during my last visit to your office in November 1997, my family has relocated to New York City. I am now under the care of a family physician, David Hart, M.D., in Manhattan. I am writing to request that you transfer my medical records to Dr. Hart at his office, 200 West 79th Street, New York, NY 10024.

Let me take this opportunity to thank you for the excellent medical care that you have given to me and my family over the past five years. I hope we are fortunate enough to receive such outstanding care in this new doctor-patient relationship.

I wish you the best in your practice.

Sincerely,

Complaint to State HMO Regulator

January 1, 1997

Insurance Commissioner
470 Atlantic Avenue
Sixth Floor
Boston, MA 02210

To the Massachusetts Insurance Commissioner:

I wish to register a complaint about ABC Health Plan, located on Route 43 in Great Barrington, MA.

I consulted with my primary care doctor, Dr. Peter Laxx, on April 15, 1997, because of severe pain in the middle of my back. Dr. Laxx prescribed painkillers and rest, but the pain did not subside. On a subsequent visit to Dr. Laxx, he suggested that since he could not see anything that would account for the severe pain, I should have a PET scan. ABC Health Plan, however, refused to cover the cost of the diagnostic test and I was unable to cover the cost out of pocket. On August 23, unable to stand the pain any longer, I went to the emergency room of Egremont Community Hospital and, after several diagnostic tests, was diagnosed with breast cancer that had spread to the lymph nodes under my right arm. I had to undergo a radical mastectomy that same day and have spent the past three months recuperating.

I feel that ABC Health Plan was fully responsible for the fact that the breast cancer was not caught early enough for me to have a less radical treatment such as a lumpectomy. I am considering a damage suit against ABC Health Plan and want to know what action you will take in the meantime.

If you require further information, I can be reached at (413) 788-6265 during the daytime and early evening.

Sincerely,

FOURTEEN

PATIENTS PRAY, HMOs PAY

Until recently, if you wanted to visit a chiropractor for a nagging back pain or a masseuse to relieve chronic headaches, you would have paid for the care yourself. Now HMOs are beginning to take a closer look at "complementary medicine" not only in response to pressure from members, but also because this emerging development may offer savings for the HMO.

Even—and perhaps especially—under traditional insurance plans, doctors have tended to have dismissive attitudes toward therapies that have come down from ancient times or haven't been proven beneficial by large-scale controlled scientific studies. The event that catapulted the medical profession into a reexamination of these treatments was the publication in 1993 of a special article in *The New England Journal of Medicine* titled "Unconventional Medicine in the United States." Written by a research team headed by Dr. Daniel M. Eisenberg, a professor at Harvard University's School of Medicine, it summarized the findings of a nationwide survey conducted in 1990. For purposes of the survey, they "limited the therapies studied to 16 medical interventions not taught widely at United States medical schools or generally available at U.S. hospitals. Examples include acupuncture, chiropractic, and massage therapy."

These findings revealed that in 1990 Americans made 425 million visits to providers of unconventional therapies, a number exceeding the 388 million visits to primary care physicians. Yet on a per-patient basis, the average number of visits to naturopathic doctors is lower than the average number of visits to conventional medical doctors. The study also found that Americans spent $13.7 million on alternative therapies, approximately $10.3 million of which was paid out of pocket.

That drain on personal pocketbooks may soon change, now that nationally renowned authorities such as Dr. Dean Ornish and Dr. Andrew Weil have shown that people definitely improve their health by changing their diets, lifestyles, and exercise patterns. Managed care organizations now acknowledge that if they can direct people to providers who do less invasive techniques and less costly techniques they will create further savings under their plans.

Some managed care plans are actually doing more than talking about it. A number of the companies, especially in California, have begun to reimburse patients for some of the treatments. At present, it is hard to know whether the move is a marketing technique on the part of companies who see that the populations they serve value the treatments or whether they actually perceive a significant clinical basis for recommendation.

Whatever the reason, HMOs are now paying for treatments that, not so long ago, they dismissed as being too unscientific. The homeopathic health care or acupuncture or massage therapy your own HMO denied payment for just a year ago may now be covered. Call the member services department of your HMO today and ask what alternative therapies your plan covers. Be sure to ask if the office will be sending an updated and current member contract to you. Ask the representative if there are any caps on the treatment coverage for each of the alternative therapies you are considering and when the coverage goes into effect. Also ask about copayments.

To maximize your benefits, it will help to build a good "case" for the role these treatments can play in improving your health and well-being. Here are some examples of how to do it:

• If you are seeing a chiropractor for relief of shoulder pains, keep a log of how often you see this alternative health care provider as well as how often you see your traditional health care provider, whether and by how much you were able to reduce visits to this conventional caregiver, and whether and by how much you were able to reduce use of pain medications.

• If you are taking stress management classes or biofeedback training to help control your ulcer attacks, keep a record of whether and by how much your attacks have been reduced and whether and by how much you have reduced your use of prescription and nonprescription medication.

• If nutritional counseling has helped you to reduce your cholesterol levels, especially low-density lipoprotein (LDL, the "bad" cholesterol), and has also raised high-density lipoprotein (HDL, the "good" cholesterol), keep an accurate record of the numbers.

• If regular yoga classes have helped you to give up sleeping pills, be sure to keep a record of the reduction in medications as well as of your improved sleeping patterns.

THE HEALER WILL SEE YOU NOW

Here are a few of the HMOs that are incorporating alternative/complementary care into their programs:

• *Blue Cross of Washington and Alaska.* A yearlong successful program in Washington State convinced Blue Cross of Washington and Alaska that a large-scale alternative health care plan would fly. It is called AlternaPath and is designed to complement patients' regular health care programs. It will cover many of the types of services usually excluded from conventional insurance programs, including those provided by naturopathic doctors, homeopathic physicians, acupuncturists, and massage therapists. The services covered by AlternaPath are intended to help subscribers suffering from health problems commonly addressed by alternative medicine, such as thyroid conditions, sinus infections, asthma, allergies, some forms of diabetes, and fibromyalgia. Blue Cross is developing the provider network in conjunction with the Alternare Group, an alternative health care consultancy based in Portland, Oregon.

- *American Western Life Insurance Company.* This California-based insurance company was a pioneer in the trend toward alternative medicine coverage. In 1993 it offered its first wellness plan, which promoted education and self-care and reimbursed for standard treatments as well as medical visits to alternative practitioners such as naturopathic physicians, chiropractors, acupuncturists, hypnotherapists, and massage therapists. A key component of the plan was the Wellness Line, a twenty-four-hour 800 number staffed by holistic doctors. Members of the plan could phone the doctors to discuss their medical conditions and receive medical information on a number of topics. The Wellness Line physicians promoted self-care for mild conditions that are treatable at home, thereby saving a visit to the doctor. In 1995 American Western launched Prevention Plus, which it called the "next generation" of health plans. Offering up to $5 million in benefits, it is a managed care plan with a flat $10 copayment for visits to conventional doctors as well as alternative practitioners. These providers include naturopathic physicians, acupuncturists, acupressurists, chiropractors, homeopathic physicians, nutritional counselors, hypnotherapists, herbalists, Ayurvedic practitioners, and yoga therapists.

- *The Alternative Health Plan.* Established in 1993, this California company's goal has been to provide medical plans that offer freedom of choice and include coverage for alternative and complementary medicine such as acupuncture, naturopathy, homeopathy, massage therapy, and other forms of alternative therapy. The plan features inpatient and outpatient coverage, holistic health care, preventive care, a transcendental meditation program, homeopathic and herbal remedies, and an optional dental plan. The plan also covers alternative and complementary therapies such as acupuncture, Ayurvedic medicine, bodywork and massage therapy, chiropractic care, herbal medicine, homeopathy, Oriental medicine, biofeedback, osteopathy, and colon therapy, as well as nutritional counseling after three months of coverage in the plan.

· *Kaiser Permanente.* The gigantic California-based organization offers alternative medicine in several clinics in Northern California. Treatment is provided in very controlled settings and is generally for management of chronic pain. The company's clinics vary in the specific types of alternative therapy offered; among them are acupuncture, acupressure, self-massage, nutritional counseling, and relaxation techniques.

· *Oxford Health Plans.* At the end of 1996, this East Coast–based managed care company launched a network of alternative care providers, starting with Connecticut, New Jersey, and New York as the first states and with Pennsylvania scheduled next. Oxford developed the plan after a company survey showed that 33 percent of its 1.5 million members in five states had used some form of alternative medicine in the prior two years. The network is made up of as many as a thousand acupuncturists, chiropractors, naturopaths, massage therapists, yoga instructors, clinical nutritionists, and registered dietitians. While Oxford's move pushed the company into the forefront of alternative medical care programs in HMOs, the company also encourages and even requires that their members see their primary care physicians.

GLOSSARY

To get the most from your health insurance benefits, it's important to understand the terms and phrases used by insurance companies or your employer. The following glossary of common terms will help you make sense out of today's rapidly changing health care industry.

Ambulatory Care Facility
A facility that provides health care services (such as surgery) on an outpatient basis, meaning an individual does not have to stay overnight. Most inpatient facilities (such as hospitals) also offer ambulatory services. Ambulatory care is sometimes called outpatient care.

Ancillary Services
Laboratory tests, X rays, and all other hospital services other than room, board, and nursing service.

Capitation
A dollar limit set by a health maintenance organization (HMO) that you or your employer pay, regardless of how much you use (or don't use) the services offered by the HMO's providers. (*Providers* is a term used for health professionals who provide care. Usually *providers* refers to doctors or hospitals. Sometimes the term also is used to refer

to nurse practitioners, chiropractors, and other health professionals who offer specialized services.)

Claim
A request by an individual (or his or her provider) to an individual's insurance company for the insurance company to pay for services received from a health care professional.

Coinsurance
Money that an individual is required to pay for services, after a deductible has been paid. In some health care plans, coinsurance is called *copayment*. Coinsurance is often specified by a percentage. For example, the employee might pay 20 percent of the charges for a service and the employer or insurance company pay the remaining 80 percent.

Copayment
A predetermined (flat) fee that an individual pays for health care services, in addition to what the insurance covers. For example, some HMOs require a $10 copayment for each visit, regardless of the type or level of services provided during the visit. Copayments are not usually specified in terms of percentages.

Deductible
The amount an individual must pay for health care expenses before insurance (or a self-insured company) covers the costs. Often, insurance plans are based on yearly deductible amounts.

Denial of Claim
Refusal by an insurance company to honor a request by an individual (or his or her provider) to pay for health care services obtained from a health care professional.

Diagnostic Related Group (DRG)
A classification system, first developed by the government for Medicare reimbursement, now used to determine the amount paid to hospitals for a patient with a certain diagnosis.

Employee Assistance Program (EAP)
A mental health counseling service that is sometimes offered by insurance companies or employers. Typically, individuals or employers do not have to pay directly for services provided through an employee assistance program.

Exclusion
A medical service that is not covered by an individual's insurance policy.

Gatekeeper
A health care provider who is the primary contact for an individual seeking medical services. The gatekeeper is usually the physician who provides basic medical services and determines whether referral to a specialist is medically appropriate and covered by the medical plan.

Health Care Financing Administration (HCFA)
The division of the Department of Health and Human Services that administers the Medicare program.

Health Maintenance Organization (HMO)
Prepaid or *capitated* insurance plans in which individuals or their employers pay a fixed monthly fee for services, instead of a separate charge for each visit or service. The monthly fees remain the same, regardless of the types or levels of services provided. Services are provided by physicians who are employed by, or under contract with, the HMO. HMOs vary in design. Depending on the type of HMO, services may be provided in a central facility or (as with IPAs described below) in a physician's own office.

Indemnity Insurance
A plan in which the individual pays a predetermined percentage of the cost of health care services, and the insurance company (or self-insured employer) pays the rest. Indemnity health insurance plans are also called *fee-for-service*. This is the type of plan that primarily existed before the rise of HMOs, IPAs, and PPOs. For example, an individual might pay 20 percent for services, and the insurance company 80 percent. The fees for services are defined by the providers and vary from

physician to physician. Indemnity health plans offer individuals the freedom to choose their health care professionals.

Independent Practice Association (IPA)
A group of health care providers for an HMO who practice in their individual offices but still follow the basic payment plans of the HMO.

Joint Commission on the Accreditation of Healthcare Organizations
A group that surveys and accredits hospitals.

Long-Term Care Policy
An insurance policy that covers specified services for a specified period of time. Long-term care policies (and their prices) vary significantly. Covered services often include nursing care, home health care services, and custodial care.

Long-Term Disability
An injury or illness that keeps a person from working for a long time period. The definition of long-term disability (and the time period over which coverage extends) differs among insurance companies and employers. Long-term disability insurance coverage is designed to protect an individual's full or partial wages during a time of injury or illness that prohibits the individual from working.

LOS
Length of stay. It is a term used by insurance companies, case managers, and/or employers to describe the amount of time an individual stays in a hospital or other inpatient facility.

Managed Care
A medical delivery system that attempts to manage the quality and cost of medical services that individuals receive. Most managed care systems offer HMOs and PPOs that individuals are encouraged to use for their health care services. Some managed care plans attempt to improve health quality by emphasizing prevention of disease.

Medicaid
A joint federal and state program that helps pay for health care for the poor and disabled. Individual states determine who is eligible for

Medicaid and which health services will be covered. Most people do not qualify for Medicaid until the majority of their money has been spent.

Medicare
The federal health care insurance program provides some medical coverage for people over sixty-five for a limited period of time. Medicare will help meet some bills for long-term care but will not fund unlimited long-term care. To meet uncovered costs, you may need supplemental, or *medigap,* insurance policies.

Maximum Dollar Limit
The maximum amount of money that an insurance company (or self-insured company) will pay for claims within a specific time period. Maximum dollar limits vary greatly. They may be based on or specified in terms of types of illnesses or types of services. Sometimes they are specified in terms of lifetime coverage, sometimes for a year.

Medigap Insurance Policy
An insurance policy offered by private insurance companies, not by the government, and designed to pay for some of the costs that Medicare does not cover. It is not the same as Medicare or Medicaid.

Open-Ended HMO
An HMO that allows enrolled individuals to use out-of-plan providers and still receive partial or full coverage and payment for the professional's services under a traditional indemnity plan.

Out-of-Plan
A phrase that usually refers to physicians, hospitals, or other health care providers who are considered nonparticipants in an insurance plan (usually an HMO or PPO). Depending on an individual's health insurance plan, expenses incurred by services provided by out-of-plan health professionals may not be covered, or may be covered only in part, by an individual's insurance company.

Out-of-Pocket Maximum
A predetermined limit on the amount of money that an individual must pay out of their own savings before an insurance company or

(self-insured employer) will pay 100 percent of an individual's health care expenses.

Outcomes Research

Research that assesses the outcomes (end results, such as ability to function, quality of life, and length of life) of individuals receiving a particular health service. Such research, for instance, would look at the percentage of people who return to normal functioning, those that partially recover, and those that die as the result of a given surgical procedure.

Outpatient

An individual (patient) who receives health care services (such as surgery) on an outpatient basis, meaning without staying overnight in a hospital or inpatient facility. Many insurance companies have identified a list of tests and procedures (including surgery) that will not be covered (paid for) unless they are performed on an outpatient basis. The term *outpatient* is used interchangeably with *ambulatory* to describe health care facilities where procedures are performed.

Preadmission Certification

Approval by a case manager or insurance company representative (usually a nurse) for a person to be admitted to a hospital or inpatient facility, granted prior to the admittance. Preadmission certification often must be obtained by the individual. Sometimes, however, physicians will contact the appropriate individual. The goal of preadmission certification is to ensure that individuals are not exposed to inappropriate health care services (services that are medically unnecessary). Also called *precertification review* and *preadmission review.*

Preadmission Review

A review of an individual's health care status or condition prior to the individual's being admitted to an inpatient health care facility such as a hospital. Preadmission reviews are often conducted by case managers or insurance company representatives (usually nurses) in cooperation with the individual, his or her physician or health care provider, and hospitals.

Preadmission Testing
Medical tests that are completed for an individual prior to admission to a hospital or inpatient health care facility.

Preexisting Condition
A medical condition that is excluded from coverage by an insurance company because the condition was believed to exist prior to the issuance of the policy.

Preferred Provider Organization (PPO)
A health care plan offering services of doctors in a preselected group. Members who use PPO doctors receive discounted rates. Members who use doctors outside the PPO plan must pay more for the medical care.

Primary Care Provider (PCP)
A health care professional (usually a physician) who is responsible for monitoring an individual's overall health care needs. Typically, a PCP serves as a "quarterback" for an individual's medical care, referring the individual to more specialized physicians for specialist care.

Provider
A health professional who provides health care services. Sometimes the term is used to refer only to physicians. Often, however, the term also refers to other health care professionals such as hospitals, nurse practitioners, chiropractors, physical therapists, and others offering specialized health care services.

Reasonable and Customary Fee
The average fee charged by a particular type of health care practitioner within a geographic area. The term is often used by medical plans to refer to the amount of money they will approve for a specific test or procedure. If the fees are higher than the approved amount, the individual receiving the service is responsible for paying the difference. Sometimes, however, if an individual questions his or her physician about the fee, the provider will reduce the charge to the amount that the insurance company has defined as reasonable and customary.

Second Opinion

A medical opinion provided by a second physician or medical expert after a first physician provides a diagnosis or recommends surgery to an individual. It is a good idea to obtain a second opinion whenever a physician recommends surgery or presents a serious medical diagnosis.

Second Surgical Opinion

An opinion provided by a second physician when a first physician recommends surgery to an individual. These are now standard benefits in many health insurance plans.

Short-Term Disability

An injury or illness that keeps a person from working for a short time. The definition of short-term disability (and the time period over which coverage extends) differs among insurance companies and employers. Short-term disability insurance coverage is designed to protect an individual's full or partial wages during a time of injury or illness (that is not work-related) that prohibits the individual from working.

Triple-Option Plan

A type of insurance plan that offers three options from which an individual may choose. Usually, the three options are: traditional indemnity, an HMO, and a PPO.

Usual, Customary, and Reasonable (UCR) Expense

An amount customarily charged for a specified service or supplies that are medically necessary, recommended by a doctor, or required for treatment. Also known as a *covered expense*.

Waiting Period

A period of time during which an individual is not covered by insurance for a particular problem.

Workers' Compensation

A network of many different state and federal laws that provide financial benefits to workers and their families as compensation for work-related injuries, illnesses, diseases, and deaths.

WHO'S WHO IN HEALTH CARE

Acupuncturist: A practitioner trained in the use of acupuncture, a procedure in which needles are used to relieve pain, increase energy, and treat nicotine and other addictions. Training and licensing of practitioners varies by state; many physicians have added acupuncture training to their arsenal of treatments.

Addictionologist: A physician who specializes in the prevention, diagnosis, and treatment of people who have a physical or emotional dependence on a substance or behavior. Addictionologists are often psychiatrists, neurologists, or internists who have received extra training in addiction medicine.

Allergist: A physician who specializes in preventing, diagnosing, and treating allergies and asthma.

Anesthesiologist: A physician who specializes in administering anesthetics and other drugs and agents that produce a complete or partial temporary loss of sensation in order to relieve pain, commonly, but not always, during surgery.

Audiologist: A health professional who diagnoses and treats hearing problems and helps provide rehabilitation to individuals with hearing loss. Audiologists must have at least a masters degree in order to qualify for practice.

Cardiologist: A physician who specializes in care of the heart.

Case Manager: A health care provider who assists an individual in assessing health and social service systems to ensure that all needed services are obtained. Case managers are frequently used in inpatient settings; they can be nurses, social workers, rehabilitation specialists, and other clinicians.

Chiropractor: A health practitioner who provides therapy based on the theory that a person's health is determined by the condition of his or her nervous system. Chiropractors cannot perform surgery or prescribe drugs. This form of treatment is largely through manual manipulation of the spine. Chiropractors earn a Doctor of Chiropractic (D.C.) after completing four years of training in an accredited chiropractic school.

Dermatologist: A physician who specializes in diseases and problems of the skin.

Dietitian: A person trained in nutritional care and eligible to be an active member of the American Dietetic Association. Registered dietitians have completed an examination and must maintain continuing education requirements.

Doula: A female practitioner experienced in childbirth who is hired as a "birth companion" to provide continuous physical, emotional, and informational support to the mother before, during, and just after childbirth.

Emergency Medical Technician (EMT): A person trained in, and responsible for, administration of specialized emergency care and transportation of acutely ill or injured individuals to a medical facility. EMTs are certified in varying levels of specialization, such as advanced life support equipment and administration of certain medications or procedures.

Emergency Medicine Physician: A physician who specializes in the rapid recognition and treatment of trauma or acute illness.

Endocrinologist: A physician who specializes in the hormonal system. Endocrinologists also specialize in the prevention, diagnosis, and treatment of diabetes mellitus.

Family Practitioner: A physician who specializes in family medicine and who often treats all members of a family, adults as well as children. Family practitioners are considered primary care physicians.

Gastroenterologist: A physician who specializes in disorders of the stomach, esophagus, intestines, and liver.

General Practitioner: A physician who is responsible for general health care needs of family members of all ages. General practitioners often serve as primary care physicians and as "gatekeepers" for an individual's health care needs, coordinating referral to other specialists when appropriate.

Geriatrician: A medical specialist in the field of geriatrics, the branch of medicine dealing with the physiology of aging.

Gynecologist: A physician who specializes in the female reproductive system.

Hematologist: A medical specialist in the field of hematology, the study of blood and blood-forming tissues.

Homeopath: A practitioner who uses techniques designed to help the body heal itself. Homeopathy follows three concepts: "like cures like," "single remedy," and "microdosage."

Immunologist: A physician who studies the reaction of immune system tissues to foreign organisms and substances.

Infectious Disease Specialist: A physician who specializes in the prevention, diagnosis, and treatment of infectious or communicable diseases—those that can be transmitted from one person to another or from animal to person, either directly or indirectly.

Infertility Specialist: A physician who specializes in the diagnosis and treatment of dysfunctions that make an individual unable to produce children.

Internist: A physician who specializes in internal medicine and cares for the physiology and pathology of the internal organs. Internists often serve as primary care physicians and as "gatekeepers" for an individual's health care needs, coordinating referral to other specialists when appropriate.

Neonatologist: A physician who specializes in the care of the infant from birth to four weeks old.

Nephrologist: A physician who cares for the kidneys.

Neurologist: A physician who specializes in the nervous system and the brain.

Nurse: A medical professional who assists physicians. Nurses may be generalists or may specialize in certain areas of care. Registered nurses (RNs) complete a course of study at an accredited school of nursing, then must pass a national licensure exam. A licensed practical nurse (LPN) is a person who has completed a training course, usually for about one year, and who is trained in basic nursing techniques. The LPN practices under the supervision of an RN.

Obstetrician: A physician who specializes in pregnancy and childbirth.

Obstetrician-Gynecologist: A physician who specializes in the female reproductive system and in pregnancy and childbirth.

Occupational Therapist (OT): A licensed health professional who treats individuals who are limited by physical injury or illness, psychosocial dysfunction, or developmental or learning disabilities.

Oncologist: A physician who specializes in the treatment of cancer.

Ophthalmologist: A physician who specializes in eye care and who performs eye surgery.

Optometrist: A professional who is trained and licensed to examine and test individuals' eyes for vision problems and to prescribe corrective lenses (eyeglasses or contact lenses). An optometrist receives a degree of Doctor of Optometry (O.D.) after successfully completing at least two years of college and four years in an approved college of optometry.

Orthopedist: A physician who specializes in the skeletal system.

Osteopath: A physician who has earned a Degree of Osteopathic Medicine (D.O.) and is licensed to practice medicine. Osteopathy is a form of physical medicine that helps restore the structural balance of the musculoskeletal system. It combines joint manipulation, physical therapy, and postural reeducation.

Otolaryngologist: A physician who specializes in the ear, nose, and throat.

Pathologist: A physician who specializes in disease and who is usually on the staff of a hospital, school of medicine, or research institution or laboratory.

Physiatrist: A physician who specializes in physical medicine and rehabilitation.

Physical Therapist (PT): A health professional licensed to help in the examination and treatment of individuals with physical limitations or disabilities. PTs have a minimum of a bachelor's degree.

Physician: A health professional who has successfully completed four years of medical school, passed a national board exam, and completed postgraduate training (an internship and/or residency) in his or her area of specialty. Licensed physicians in the U.S. have earned either a degree of Doctor of Medicine (M.D.) or of Doctor of Osteopathic Medicine (D.O.). Physicians are licensed to prescribe medications and treatments.

Podiatrist: A health professional who specializes in care of the feet. Podiatrists complete a four-year postgraduate program leading to a degree of Doctor of Podiatric Medicine.

Proctologist: A physician who specializes in treatment of the colon, rectum, and anus.

Psychiatrist: A physician who specializes in mental, emotional, and behavioral disorders. They have a medical degree and specialty training and are the only mental health specialists who can prescribe medication.

Psychologist: A person who studies human behavior. A clinical psychologist holds a graduate degree in psychology (Ph.D.), and provides counseling to people with mental or emotional disorders.

Pulmonologist: A physician who specializes in disorders of the lung.

Radiologist: A physician who specializes in the diagnosis and treatment of disease using various types of radiant electromagnetic energy, such as X rays.

Rheumatologist: A physician who specializes in connective tissue and related structures; largely, they diagnose and treat inflamed and diseased joints and arthritis.

Speech/Language Pathologist: A person with graduate professional training in human communication, its development, and related disorders. Speech-language pathologists measure and evaluate language abilities, hearing processes, and how speech is produced, and treat children and adults who have speech, language, and hearing disorders.

Thoracic Surgeon: A physician who performs chest and lung surgery.

Urologist: A physician who specializes in treatment of the urinary tract in males and females and the genital tract in males, including prostate problems.

Vascular Surgeon: A physician who specializes in the surgical treatment of arteries or veins.

STATE HMO REGULATORS

ALABAMA

Alabama Department of Public
    Health
Director, Life and Health
434 Monroe Street
Montgomery, AL 36130
Tel: 205-613-5366

Department of Insurance
Insurance Commissioner
135 South Union Street
Montgomery, AL 36130
Tel: 205-269-3550

ALASKA

Department of Insurance
Director of Insurance
PO Box 110805
333 Willoughby Avenue,
    9th Floor
Juneau, AK 99811
Tel: 602-912-8400

ARIZONA

Department of Insurance
2910 North 44th Street, Suite 210
Phoenix, AZ 85012
Tel: 602-912-8400

ARKANSAS

Arkansas Insurance Department
400 University Tower Building
1123 South University Avenue
Little Rock, AR 72204
Tel: 501-686-2900

CALIFORNIA

Department of Corporations
Commissioner of Corporations
3700 Wilshire Boulevard, Suite
    600
Los Angeles, CA 90010
Tel: 213-736-3481

Department of Corporations
Commissioner of Corporations
1115 11th Street
Sacramento, CA 95814
Tel: 916-654-8076

Insurance Department
Insurance Commissioner
1120 One City Centre Building
770 L Street
Sacramento, CA 95814
Tel: 916-324-9020

COLORADO

Division of Insurance
1560 Broadway, Suite 850
Denver, CO 80202
Tel: 303-894-7499

CONNECTICUT

Department of Insurance
PO Box 816
153 Market Street, 11th Floor
Hartford, CT 06142
Tel: 203-297-3800

Commission of Hospitals and
    Health Care
1049 Asylum Avenue
Hartford, CT 06105
Tel: 203-566-3880

DELAWARE

Department of Insurance
841 Silver Lake Boulevard
Dover, DE 19901
Tel: 302-739-4251

Department of Public Health,
    Health Facilities, Licenses and
    Certification
3 Mill Road, Suite 308
Wilmington, DE 19806
Tel: 302-577-6666

DISTRICT OF COLUMBIA

Department of Insurance
    Administration
441 Fourth Street NW, Suite 931
Washington, DC 20001
Tel: 202-727-8000

FLORIDA

Florida Department of Insurance
Bureau of Specialty Insurers
200 East Gaines Street
Tallahassee, FL 32399
Tel: 904-922-3131

GEORGIA

Licensing Department
Georgia Department of
    Insurance
704 West Tower
Floyd Memorial Building
2 Martin Luther King, Jr. Drive
Atlanta, GA 30334
Tel: 404-656-2056

HAWAII

Department of Health, State
    Planning and Development
335 Merchant Street, Room 214
    East
Honolulu, HI 96813
Tel: 808-587-0788

State Insurance Department
Insurance Commissioner
250 South King Street, 5th Floor
Honolulu, HI 96813
Tel: 808-586-2790

IDAHO

Department of Insurance
Insurance Director
700 West State Street, 3rd Floor
Boise, ID 83720
Tel: 208-334-2250

ILLINOIS

Illinois Department of Insurance
HMO Compliance Unit
320 West Washington Street,
    4th Floor
Springfield, IL 62767
Tel: 217-782-4515

Department of Public Health
Director of Health
535 West Jefferson Street,
    Room 500
Springfield, IL 62761
Tel: 217-782-4977

INDIANA

Indiana Department of Insurance
311 West Washington Street,
    Suite 300
Indianapolis, IN 46204
Tel: 317-232-2395

IOWA

Division of Insurance
Lucas State Office Building
Des Moines, IA 50319
Tel: 515-281-5705

Life and Health Department
Bureau Chief
Lucas State Office Building
Des Moines, IA 50319
Tel: 515-281-4222

KANSAS

Kansas Insurance Department
420 SW 9th Street
Topeka, KS 66612
Tel: 913-296-3071

KENTUCKY

Division of Licensing and
    Regulation, Cabinet for
    Human Resources
CHR Building, 4th Floor
275 East Main Street
Frankfort, KY 40621
Tel: 502-564-2800

Department of Insurance, Life
    and Health Division
PO Box 517
215 West Main Street
Frankfort, KY 40601
Tel: 502-564-3630

Department of Insurance
Financial Standards and
    Examination Division
PO Box 517
215 West Main Street
Frankfort, KY 40601
Tel: 502-564-6082

LOUISIANA

Department of Insurance
950 North Fifth Street
Baton Rouge, LA 70802
Tel: 504-342-5301

MAINE

Bureau of Insurance
Department of Professional and
    Financial Regulation
State House, Station 34
Augusta, ME 04333
Tel: 207-582-8707

MARYLAND

Department of Licensing and
    Regulation
Insurance Division
Stanblat Building, 7th Floor
    South
501 St. Paul Place
Baltimore, MD 21202
Tel: 410-333-2770

Life and Health Section
Maryland Insurance
    Administration
501 St. Paul Place
Baltimore, MD 20202
Tel: 410-333-6104

MASSACHUSETTS

Massachusetts Division of
    Insurance
470 Atlantic Avenue
Boston, MA 02210
Tel: 617-521-7349

MICHIGAN

Department of Commerce
Michigan Insurance Bureau
PO Box 30220
Lansing, MI 48909
Tel: 517-373-0240

Michigan Department of Public
    Health
3423 Martin Luther King
    Boulevard
Lansing, MI 48909
Tel: 517-335-8551

Department of Insurance
Insurance Commissioner
611 West Ottawa Street, 2nd
    Floor North
Lansing, MI 48933
Tel: 517-373-9273

MINNESOTA

Minnesota Department of Health
Occupational and Systems
    Compliance Division
Managed Care Systems Section
121 East 7th Place, Suite 400
St. Paul, MN 55101
Tel: 612-282-5614

State Insurance Department
Insurance Commissioner
133 East 7th Place
St. Paul, MN 55101
Tel: 612-296-6848

MISSISSIPPI

State Health Department
Division of Licensure and
    Certification
421 West Pascagoula Street
Jackson, MS 39204
Tel: 601-354-7300

State Department of Insurance
Insurance Commissioner
1804 Walter Sillers Building
Jackson, MS 39204
Tel: 601-354-7300

MISSOURI

Department of Insurance
301 West High Street, Room 630
Jefferson City, MO 65101
Tel: 314-751-2640

MONTANA

Insurance Department
Commissioner of Insurance
270 Mitchell Building
126 North Sanders
Helena, MT 59620
Tel: 406-444-2040

NEBRASKA

Department of Insurance
941 O Street, Suite 400
Lincoln, NE 68508
Tel: 402-471-2201

NEVADA

Department of Business and
    Industry
Division of Insurance
1665 Hot Springs Road, Suite 152
Carson City, NV 89716
Tel: 702-687-4270

NEW HAMPSHIRE

Department of Insurance
169 Manchester Street
Concord, NH 03301
Tel: 603-271-2261

NEW JERSEY

Department of Health
Division of Health Facilities
    Evaluation and Licensing
CN-367
Trenton, NJ 08625
Tel: 609-588-7725

Department of Health
Alternative Health Systems
CN-367
Trenton, NJ 08625
Tel: 609-588-2510

Department of Insurance
Division of Actuarial Services,
    Life and Health
Managed Healthcare Bureau
CN-325
20 West State Street
Trenton, NJ 08625
Tel: 609-292-5363

New Mexico

New Mexico Department of
Insurance
PO Drawer 1269
Santa Fe, NM 87501
Tel: 505-827-4500

New York

Department of Insurance
Health and Life Policy Bureau
Agency Building 1
Empire State Plaza
Albany, NY 12257
Tel: 518-474-4098

New York State Department of
Health
Bureau of Alternative Delivery
Systems
Corning Tower, Room 1911
Albany, NY 12237
Tel: 518-473-8944

New York State Department of
Health
Bureau of Management Analysis
Records Access Office
Corning Tower, Room 2230
Albany, NY 12237
Tel: 518-474-8734

North Carolina

Department of Insurance
Managed Care and Health
Benefits Division
112 Cox Avenue
Raleigh, NC 17605
Tel: 919-715-0526

Department of Insurance
Financial Compliance Division
430 North Salisbury Street
Raleigh, NC 27605
Tel: 919-733-5633

Department of Insurance
Life and Health Division
430 North Salisbury Street
Raleigh, NC 27605
Tel: 919-733-5060

Department of Insurance
Consumer Services Division
PO Box 26387
Raleigh, NC 27605
Tel: 919-733-2004

North Dakota

Department of Insurance
State Capitol
600 East Boulevard
Bismarck, ND 58505
Tel: 701-224-2440

Ohio

Department of Insurance
Managed Care Division
2100 Stella Court
Columbus, OH 43266
Tel: 614-644-2661

Oklahoma

State Department of Health
Special Health Services
1000 NE 10th Street
Oklahoma City, OK 73117
Tel: 405-271-6868

State Department of Insurance
Insurance Commissioner
1901 North Walnut
Oklahoma City, OK 73152
Tel: 405-521-2828

OREGON

Department of Consumer and
  Business Services
Insurance Division 440-4
Labor and Industries Building
Salem, OR 97310
Tel: 503-378-4271

Department of Consumer and
  Business Services
470 Labor and Industries
  Building
Salem, OR 97310
Tel: 503-378-4481/4484

PENNSYLVANIA

Department of Insurance
Insurance Commissioner
1321 Strawberry Square
Harrisburg, PA 17120
Tel: 717-787-2317/5173/5890

Department of Health
Bureau of Healthcare Financing
Box 90
Health and Welfare Building,
  Room 1026
Harrisburg, PA 17108
Tel: 717-787-5193

Department of Insurance
1400 Spring Garden Street,
  Room 1701
Philadelphia, PA 19130
Tel: 215-560-2630

Pennsylvania Insurance
  Department
300 Liberty Avenue
304 State Office Building
Pittsburgh, PA 15222
Tel: 412-565-5020

Erie Regional Office
Pennsylvania Insurance
  Department
PO Box 6142
Baldwin Building, Room 513
Erie, PA 16512
Tel: 814-871-4466

PUERTO RICO

Department of Insurance
Insurance Commissioner
Fernandez Juncos Station
1607 Ponce de Leon Avenue
Santurce, PR 00910
Tel: 809-722-8686

RHODE ISLAND

Division of Insurance
Department of Business
  Regulation
233 Richmond Street, Suite 233
Providence, RI 02903
Tel: 401-277-2223

SOUTH CAROLINA

Insurance Commission
1612 Marion Street
Columbia, SC 29201
Tel: 803-737-6221

Insurance Commission
Department of Insurance
PO Box 100105
Columbus, SC 29201
Tel: 803-737-6150/6160

South Dakota

Department of Health
445 East Capitol Avenue
Pierre, SD 57501
Tel: 605-773-3361

State Department of Insurance
Insurance Director
500 East Capitol
Pierre, SD 57501
Tel: 605-773-3563

Tennessee

Department of Health
Division of Health Care Facilities
283 Plus Park Boulevard
Nashville, TN 37247
Tel: 615-367-6316

Department of Commerce and
    Insurance
Policy Holders Service Section
500 James Robertson Parkway
Nashville, TN 37243
Tel: 800-342-4029

Texas

Texas Department of Insurance
PO Box 149104
333 Guadalupe Street
Austin, TX 78714
Tel: 512-463-6500/6515;
    800-252-3439

Texas Department of Health
Director, Health Department
1100 West 49th Street
Austin, TX 78756
Tel: 512-322-4266

Utah

State Insurance Department
State Office Building, Suite 3110
Salt Lake City, UT 84114
Tel: 801-538-3800/3805

Vermont

Department of Banking,
    Insurance and Securities
89 Main Street, Drawer 20
Montpelier, VT 05620
Tel: 802-828-3301

Virginia

State Corporation Commission
Bureau of Insurance
Box 1157
1300 East Main Street
Richmond, VA 23219
Tel: 804-371-9691

Washington

Office of the Insurance
    Commissioner
Insurance Building
PO Box 40255
Olympia, WA 98504
Tel: 206-753-7301

Office of the Insurance
  Commissioner
Consumer Protection
PO Box 40256
Olympia, WA 98504
Tel: 206-753-3613

WEST VIRGINIA

Insurance Commission Office
2019 Washington Street, E
Charleston, WV 23540
Tel: 304-558-3386

WISCONSIN

Office of the Commissioner of
  Insurance
121 East Wilson
Madison, WI 53703
Tel: 608-266-0103

WYOMING

Wyoming Insurance Department
122 West 25th Street
Cheyenne, WY 82002
Tel: 307-777-7401

APPENDIX B

STATE PHYSICIAN REGULATORS

ALABAMA

Alabama Board of Medical
    Examiners
PO Box 946
Montgomery, AL 36101
Tel: 205-242-4116

ALASKA

Alaska State Medical Association
4107 Laurel Street
Anchorage, AL 99508
Tel: 907-562-2662

ARIZONA

Arizona Board of Medical
    Examiners
2001 West Camelback Road,
    Suite 300
Phoenix, AZ 85012
Tel: 602-255-3751

ARKANSAS

Arkansas State Medical Board
2100 Riverfront Drive, Suite 200
Little Rock, AR 72202
Tel: 501-296-1802

CALIFORNIA

California Medical Board
1426 Howe Avenue, Suite 54
Sacramento, CA 95825-3236
Tel: 916-263-2499

COLORADO

Colorado Board of Medical
    Examiners
1560 Broadway, Suite 1300
Denver, CO 80202-5140
Tel: 303-894-7690

CONNECTICUT

Department of Public Health and
   Administration
Licensure and Registration
150 Washington Street
Hartford, CT 06106
Tel: 203-566-5296

Department of Health Service
Hearing Office
150 Washington Street
Hartford, CT 06106
Tel: 203-566-1011

DELAWARE

Board of Medical Practice of
   Delaware
Division of Professional
   Regulation
PO Box 1401
Margaret O'Neill Building,
   2nd Floor
Dover, DE 19903
Tel: 302-739-4522

DISTRICT OF COLUMBIA

District of Columbia Board of
   Medicine
Department of Consumer Affairs
605 H Street NW, Suite 931
Washington, DC 20001
Tel: 202-727-8000

FLORIDA

Florida Board of Medicine
1940 North Monroe Street
Tallahassee, FL 32399
Tel: 904-488-0595

GEORGIA

Composite State Board of
   Medical Examiners
166 Pryor Street South West
Atlanta, GA 30303
Tel: 404-656-3913

HAWAII

Board of Medical Examiners
Professional Vocational Division
PO Box 3469
Honolulu, HI 96801
Tel: 808-586-2677

IDAHO

Idaho State Board of Medical
   Examiners
PO Box 83720
Boise, ID 83720-0058
Tel: 208-334-2822

ILLINOIS

Illinois Department of
   Professional Regulation
320 West Washington Street,
   3rd Floor
Springfield, IL 62786
Tel: 217-785-0820

INDIANA

Medical Licensing Board of
   Indiana
Health Professions Bureau
Records Division, Room 041
402 West Washington Street
Indianapolis, IN 46204
Tel: 317-233-4432

Department of Insurance
311 West Washington Street,
    Suite 300
Indianapolis, IN 46204
Tel: 317-232-5065/5430

IOWA

Iowa State Board of Medical
    Examiners
State Capital Complex
Executive Hills West
Des Moines, IA 50319
Tel: 515-281-4115

KANSAS

Kansas State Board of Healing
    Arts
235 South Topeka Boulevard
Topeka, KS 66603
Tel: 913-296-7413

KENTUCKY

Kentucky Medical Licensure
    Board
310 Whittington Parkway,
    Suite 1B
Louisville, KY 40222
Tel: 502-429-8046

LOUISIANA

Louisiana State Board of Medical
    Examiners
830 Union Street, Suite 100
New Orleans, LA 70112
Tel: 504-524-6763

MAINE

Board of Licensure and Medicine
2 Bangor Street
State House, Station 137
Augusta, ME 04333
Tel: 207-287-3601

MARYLAND

Board of Physician Quality
    Assurance
4201 West Patterson Avenue
Baltimore, MD 21215
Tel: 410-764-4777

MASSACHUSETTS

Board of Registration in
    Medicine
10 West Street
Boston, MA 02111
Tel: 617-727-3086

MICHIGAN

Michigan Board of Medicine
Box 30018
611 West Ottawa Street
Lansing, MI 48909
Tel: 517-373-6873

MINNESOTA

Minnesota Board of Medical
    Practice
2700 University Avenue,
    W. Suite 106
St. Paul, MN 55114
Tel: 612-642-0538

MISSISSIPPI

State Medical Licensure Board
2688 D Insurance Center Drive
Jackson, MS 39216
Tel: 601-354-6645

MISSOURI

Missouri State Board of
  Registration for the
  Healing Arts
3605 Missouri Boulevard, Box 4
Jefferson City, MO 65102
Tel: 314-751-0098

MONTANA

Professional and Occupational
  Licensing
Board of Medical Examiners
111 North Jackson, Box 200513
Helena, MT 59620-0513
Tel: 406-444-4276

NEBRASKA

Bureau of Examining Boards
301 Centennial Mall South
Lincoln, NE 68509-5009
Tel: 402-471-2115

NEVADA

Nevada State Board of Medical
  Examiners
PO Box 7238
Reno, NV 89510
Tel: 702-688-2559

NEW HAMPSHIRE

New Hampshire Board of
  Registration in Medicine
2 Industrial Park Drive, Suite 8
Concord, NH 03301-8520
Tel: 603-271-1203

NEW JERSEY

Board of Medical Examiners
140 East Front Street
Trenton, NJ 08608
Tel: 609-826-7100

NEW MEXICO

New Mexico Board of Medical
  Examiners
491 Old Santa Fe Trail
Lamy Building, 2nd Floor
Santa Fe, MN 87501
Tel: 505-827-7317

NEW YORK

New York State Department of
  Health
Corning Tower
Empire State Plaza
Albany, NY 12237
Tel: 518-474-8357

NORTH CAROLINA

North Carolina Board of Medical
  Examiners
PO Box 20007
Raleigh, NC 27609
Tel: 919-828-1212

North Dakota

North Dakota State Board of
  Medical Examiners
City Center Plaza
418 East Broadway Avenue, Suite
  12
Bismarck, ND 58505
Tel: 701-223-9485

Ohio

State Medical Board of Ohio
77 South High Street, 17th Floor
Columbus, OH 43266-0315
Tel: 614-466-3934

Oklahoma

Oklahoma State Board of
  Medical Licensure and
  Supervision
PO Box 18256
Oklahoma City, OK 73154-0256
Tel: 405-271-6868

Oregon

Board of Medical Examiners
1500 South West 1st Avenue,
  Suite 620
Portland, OR 97201-5826
Tel: 503-229-5770

Pennsylvania

State Board of Medicine
PO Box 2649
Harrisburg, PA 17105
Tel: 717-783-1400

Rhode Island

Rhode Island Department of
  Health
Rhode Island Board of Medical
  Licensure and Discipline
3 Capitol Hill
Providence, RI 12908
Tel: 401-277-3855

South Carolina

State Board of Medical
  Examiners of South Carolina
101 Executive Center Drive
Saluda Building, Suite 120
PO Box 212269
Columbia, SC 29221-2269

South Dakota

State Board of Medical and
  Osteopathic Examiners
1323 South Minnesota Avenue
Sioux Falls, SD 57105
Tel: 605-336-1965

Tennessee

Department of Health
Health Related Boards
344 Cordell Hull Building
Nashville, TN 37247
Tel: 615-367-6220

Texas

Department of Health
State Board of Medical
  Examiners
1100 West 49th Street
Austin, TX 78756
Tel: 512-834-7728

UTAH

Business Regulation
Division of Occupational and
    Professional Licensing
PO Box 45805
160 East 300th South
Salt Lake City, UT 84145
Tel: 801-530-6628

VERMONT

Secretary of State Office
Board of Medical Practice
109 State Street
Montpelier, VT 05609-1106
Tel: 802-828-2673

VIRGINIA

Board of Medicine
Department of Health
    Professions
6606 West Broad Street, 4th Floor
Richmond, VA 23230-1717
Tel: 804-662-9925

WASHINGTON

Department of Health
PO Box 47866
Olympia, WA 98504-7866
Tel: 206-753-2287

WEST VIRGINIA

West Virginia Board of Medicine
101 Dee Drive
Charleston, WV 25311
Tel: 304-558-2921

WISCONSIN

Wisconsin Medical Examining
    Board
PO Box 8935
1400 East Washington Avenue
Madison, WI 53708
Tel: 608-266-2811

WYOMING

Wyoming Board of Medicine
Barrett Building, 2nd Floor
Cheyenne, WY 82002
Tel: 307-777-6463

STATE HOSPITAL REGULATORS

ALABAMA

Alabama Department of Public
  Health
Division of Licensure and
  Certification
434 Monroe Street
Montgomery, AL 36130
Tel: 205-240-3503

State Health and Planning
  Development Agencies
312 Montgomery Street, 7th floor
Montgomery, AL 36104
Tel: 205-242-4103

ALASKA

Health Facility Certification and
  Licensing
4796-6 Business Park Boulevard
Building H
Anchorage, AL 99503
Tel: 907-561-8081

ARIZONA

Arizona Department of Health
  Services
Division of EMS/Health Care
  Facilities
Office of Health Care Licensure
100 West Clarendon, 4th Floor
Phoenix, AZ 85013
Tel: 602-255-1177

ARKANSAS

Department of Health
Division of Health Facility
  Services
4815 West Markham Street, Mail
  Slot 9
Little Rock, AR 72205-3867

CALIFORNIA

Licensing and Certification
  Headquarters
PO Box 942732
1800 Third Street, Suite 210
Sacramento, CA 94234
Tel: 916-327-7015

Sacramento District
  916-387-2500

Chico District
  916-895-6711

Santa Rosa District
  707-576-2380

Berkeley District
  310-540-2417

Daly City District
  415-301-9971

San Jose District
  408-277-1784

Fresno District
  209-445-5168

Ventura District
  805-654-4800

Orange County District
  714-558-4001

San Diego District
  619-688-6190

San Bernardino District
  909-383-4777

Los Angeles District
  213-351-8200

COLORADO

Department of Health
Department of Health Facilities
4300 Cherry Creek Drive South
Denver, CO 80222-15300
Tel: 303-692-2000

CONNECTICUT

Connecticut State Department of
  Public Health and Addiction
  Services
Division of Hospital and Medical
  Care
150 Washington Street
Hartford, CT 06106
Tel: 860-566-5758

DELAWARE

Department of Health Facilities
  Licensing and Certification
3 Mill Road, Suite 308
Wilmington, DE 19806
Tel: 302-577-6666

Peer Health Planning and
  Resource Management
Delaware Health Statistics
  Center
PO Box 637
Jesse Cooper Building
Dover, DE 19903
Tel: 302-739-4776

DISTRICT OF COLUMBIA

Occupational and Professional
  Licensing Administration
License and Certification
  Division
614 H Street NW, Suite 931
Washington, DC 20001
Tel: 202-727-8000

FLORIDA

Agency for Healthcare
    Administration
Hospital Unit
2727 Mahan Drive
Tallahassee, FL 32308
Tel: 904-487-2717

Agency for Healthcare
    Administration
Certification of Need Office
2727 Mahan Drive
Tallahassee, FL 32308
Tel: 904-488-8673

Agency for Healthcare
    Administration
State Center for Health Statistics,
    Research and Analysis
Atrium Building, Suite 301
325 John Knox Road
Tallahassee, FL 32303
Tel: 904-922-3131

GEORGIA

Department of Human
    Resources
Office of Regulatory Services
Health Care Section
2 Peachtree Street NW, 19th Floor
Atlanta, GA 30303
Tel: 404-657-5550

HAWAII

Department of Health
Hospital and Medical Facilities
Medicare Section
1270 Queen Emma Street, Suite
    1100
Honolulu, HI 96813
Tel: 808-586-4077

IDAHO

Department of Health and
    Welfare
Bureau of Facility Standards,
    Licensing and Certification
Statehouse Mall
450 West State Street, 2nd Floor
Boise, ID 83720
Tel: 208-334-6626

Office of Health Policy and
    Resource Development
Division of Health
Idaho Department of Health and
    Welfare
450 West State Street, 4th Floor
Boise, ID 83720
Tel: 208-334-5992

ILLINOIS

Illinois Department of Public
    Health
535 West Jefferson Street
Springfield, IL 62761
Tel: 217-786-7001

Health Care Cost Containment
4500 South 6th Street Road
Springfield, IL 62703
Tel: 217-786-7001

INDIANA

Indiana State Department of
    Health
Division of Acute Care
1330 West Michigan Street,
    Room 336
Indianapolis, IN 46202
Tel: 317-633-8400

Iowa

Department of Inspections and
    Appeals
Health Facilities
Lucas State Office Building
Des Moines, IA 50319
Tel: 515-281-5705

Kansas

Bureau of Adult and Child Care
Kansas Department of Health
    and Environment
Landon State Office Building,
    Suite 1001
900 SW Jackson
Topeka, KS 66612-1290
Tel: 913-296-1240

Kansas Department of Health
    and Environment
Research and Analysis
    Department
109 SW 9th Street
Mills Building, Suite 400A
Topeka, KS 66612-2219
Tel: 913-296-5645

Kentucky

Division of Licensing and
    Regulation, Cabinet for
    Human Resources
CHR Building, 4th Floor
275 East Main Street
Frankfort, KY 40621
Tel: 502-564-2800

Division of Licensing and
    Regulation
Health Data Branch
275 East Main Street
Frankfort, KY 40621
Tel: 502-564-2757

Louisiana

Department of Health and
    Hospitals
Bureau of Health Services
    Financing
Health Standards Section
PO Box 3767
Baton Rouge, LA 70821
Tel: 504-342-5900

Maine

Division of Licensing and
    Certification
Department of Human Services
State House, Station 11
Augusta, ME 04333
Tel: 207-624-5443

Maryland

Licensing and Certification
    Programs
4201 West Patterson Avenue
Baltimore, MD 21215
Tel: 410-764-2750

Health Services Cost Review
    Commission
4201 West Patterson Avenue
Baltimore, MD 21215
Tel: 410-764-2605

Maryland Health Resources
　　Planning Commission
4201 West Patterson Avenue
Baltimore, MD 21215
Tel: 410-764-3255

MASSACHUSETTS

Division of Health Care Quality
Department of Public Health
10 West Street, 5th Floor
Boston, MA 02111
Tel: 617-727-5860

Bureau of Health Statistics,
　　Research and Evaluation
Massachusetts Department of
　　Public Health
150 Tremont Street, 8th Floor
Boston, MA 02111
Tel: 617-727-6452

MICHIGAN

Division of Licensing and
　　Certification
3500 North Logan Street
Lansing, MI 48909
Tel: 517-335-8505

MINNESOTA

Minnesota Department of Health
Health Resources Division
PO Box 54900
Central Medical Building
393 North Dunlap
St. Paul, MN 55164-0900
Tel: 612-643-2149

MISSISSIPPI

State Health Department
Division of Health Facility
　　Licensure and Certification
PO Box 1700
Jackson, MS 39215
Tel: 601-354-7300

MISSOURI

Department of Health
Bureau of Licensing and
　　Certification
PO Box 570
Jefferson City, MO 65102
Tel: 314-751-6279

MONTANA

Bureau of Licensing and
　　Certification
Health Facilities Division
W. F. Cogswell Building
Helena, MT 59620
Tel: 406-444-2676

Health Services Division
Health Planning Program
W. F. Cogswell Building,
　　Room C216
Helena, MT 59620
Tel: 406-444-5268

NEBRASKA

Department of Health
Bureau of Health Facilities
　　Standards
301 Centennial Mall South
Lincoln, NE 68509-5007
Tel: 402-471-2946

NEVADA

Bureau of Licensure and
  Certification
Nevada Health Division
505 East King, Suite 202
Carson City, NV 89710
Tel: 702-687-4475

NEW HAMPSHIRE

Bureau of Health Facilities
  Administration
6 Hazen Drive
Concord, NH 03301
Tel: 603-271-4592

NEW JERSEY

Department of Health
Division of Health Facilities
  Evaluation and Licensing
CN-367
Trenton, NJ 08625
Tel: 609-588-7725

NEW MEXICO

Department of Health
Health Facility Licensing and
  Certification Bureau
525 Camino De Los Marquez,
  Suite 2
Santa Fe, NM 87501
Tel: 505-827-4200

Health Policy Commission
410 Don Gaspar
Santa Fe, NM 87501
Tel: 505-827-4488

NEW YORK

Office of Health Systems
  Management
Tower Building
Empire State Plaza
Albany, NY 12237-0701
Tel: 518-474-7028

New York State Department of
  Health
Bureau of Biometrics
Concourse Room C-144
Empire State Plaza
Albany, NY 12237
Tel: 518-474-3189

NORTH CAROLINA

Division of Facility Services
Licensure Section, Acute Care
  Branch
PO Box 29530
Raleigh, NC 27626-0530
Tel: 919-733-1604

Medical Database Commission
112 Cox Avenue
Raleigh, NC 27605
Tel: 919-733-7141

NORTH DAKOTA

Division of Health Facilities
North Dakota Department of
  Health
600 East Boulevard
Bismarck, ND 58505
Tel: 701-224-2352

OHIO

Ohio Department of Health
Office of Resources Development
246 North High Street
Columbus, OH 43266-0588
Tel: 614-466-3325

Ohio Department of Health
Office of Health Policy
246 North High Street
Columbus, OH 43268-0588
Tel: 614-644-1912

OKLAHOMA

State Department of Health
1000 NE 10th Street
Oklahoma City, OK 73117-1299
Tel: 405-271-6868

State Department of Health
Health Planning
1000 NE 10th Street
Oklahoma City, OK 73117-1299
Tel: 405-271-3943

OREGON

Oregon Health Division
Health Care Licensing and
    Certification
PO Box 14450
Portland, OR 97214
Tel: 503-731-4013

Office of Health Policy
Suite 640
800 North East Oregon Street,
    No. 23
Portland, OR 97232
Tel: 503-731-4091

PENNSYLVANIA

Division of Hospitals
Health and Welfare Building,
    Suite 532
Harrisburg, PA 17120
Tel: 717-783-8980

Pennsylvania Health
    Department
Division of Health Statistics and
    Research
State Center
PO Box 90
Harrisburg, PA 17108
Tel: 717-783-2548

RHODE ISLAND

Rhode Island Department of
    Health
Division of Facilities Regulation
3 Capitol Hill
Providence RI 02908
Tel: 401-277-2566

SOUTH CAROLINA

Department of Health and
    Environmental Control
Bureau of Health Regulations
2600 Bull Street
Columbia, SC 29201
Tel: 803-737-7202

Department of Health and
    Environmental Control
Bureau of Health Facilities and
    Services Development
2600 Bull Street
Columbia, SC 29201
Tel: 803-737-7200

SOUTH DAKOTA

Licensure and Certification
  Program
South Dakota Department of
  Health
Joe Foss Building
523 East Capitol Avenue
Pierre, SD 57501
Tel: 605-773-3364

South Dakota Department of
  Health
Policy and Statistics
445 East Capitol Avenue
Pierre, SD 57501
Tel: 605-773-3361

TENNESSEE

Division for Licensing Health
  Care Facilities
283 Plus Park Boulevard
Nashville, TN 37247-0508
Tel: 615-367-6303

TEXAS

Health Facility Licensure and
  Certification
Texas Department of Health
1100 West 49th Street
Austin, TX 78756
Tel: 512-834-6650

Bureau of State Health Data
  Policy Analysis
Texas Department of Health
1100 West 49th Street
Austin, TX 78756
Tel: 512-458-7261

Disclosure Section
Texas Department of Health
1100 West 49th Street
Austin, TX 78756
Tel: 512-834-6687

UTAH

Utah Department of Health
Bureau of Health Facility
  Licensure
PO Box 16990
288 North 1460 West
Salt Lake City, UT 84116-0900
Tel: 801-538-6152

VERMONT

Vermont Department of Health
Division of Public Health
  Analysis Policy
108 Cherry Street
PO Box 70
Burlington, VT 05402
Tel: 802-863-7300

VIRGINIA

Office of Health Facilities
  Regulation
Department of Health
3600 West Broad Street, Suite 216
Richmond, VA 23230
Tel: 804-367-2102

Center for Health Statistics
PO Box 1000
Richmond, VA 23208
Tel: 804-786-6206

WASHINGTON

Department of Health
Facilities and Services Licensing
PO Box 47852
Olympia, WA 98504-7852
Tel: 206-705-6652

Department of Health
Office of Hospital Patient Data
   Systems
1102 South East Quince Street
PO Box 47811
Olympia, WA 98504-7811
Tel: 206-705-6003

WEST VIRGINIA

Office of Health Facility
   Licensure and Certification
West Virginia Division of Health
State Capitol Complex
1900 Kanawha Boulevard E
Building 3, Room 550
Charleston, WV 25305
Tel: 304-558-0050

West Virginia Healthcare Cost
   Review Authority
100 Dee Drive, Suite 201
Charleston, WV 25311
Tel: 304-558-7000

WISCONSIN

Bureau of Quality Compliance
Department of Health and Social
   Services
PO Box 309
Madison, WI 53701
Tel: 608-266-8481

Office of Commissioner of
   Insurance
Office of Healthcare Information
121 East Wilson Street, 1st Floor
Madison, WI 53702
Tel: 608-267-0236

WYOMING

Health Facilities Licensing Unit
Department of Health
Hathaway Building, 4th Floor
2300 Capitol Avenue
Cheyenne, WY 82002
Tel: 307-777-7123

STATE INSURANCE
HELP LINES

Alabama
800-243-5463

Alaska
800-478-6065
907-562-7249

Arizona
800-432-4040

Arkansas
800-852-5494
501-686-2940

California
800-927-4357
916-323-7315

Colorado
303-894-7499

Connecticut
800-443-9946

Delaware
800-336-9500

District of Columbia
202-676-3900

Florida
904-922-2073

Georgia
800-669-8387

Hawaii
808-586-0100

Idaho
800-247-4422

Illinois
800-252-8966

Indiana
800-452-4800

Iowa
515-281-5705

Kansas
800-432-3535

Kentucky
800-372-2991

Louisiana
800-259-5301

Maine
800-750-5353

Maryland
800-243-3425

Massachusetts
800-882-2003

Michigan
517-373-8230

Minnesota
800-882-6262

Mississippi
800-948-3090

Missouri
800-390-3330

Montana
800-332-2272

Nebraska
402-471-4506

Nevada
800-307-4444

New Hampshire
603-271-4642

New Jersey
800-792-8820

New Mexico
800-432-2080

New York
800-333-4114

North Carolina
800-443-9354

North Dakota
800-686-1578

Oklahoma
405-521-6628

Oregon
800-722-4134

Pennsylvania
717-783-8975

Puerto Rico
809-721-5710

Rhode Island
800-322-2880

South Carolina
800-868-9095

South Dakota
605-773-3656

Tennessee
800-525-2816

Texas
800-252-3439

Utah
801-538-3910

Vermont
800-642-5119

Virginia
800-552-3402

Virgin Islands
809-774-2991

Washington
800-397-4422

West Virginia
304-558-3317

Wisconsin
800-242-1060

Wyoming
800-438-5768

MEDICAL SPECIALTY BOARDS

Twenty-four medical specialties are board certified by the American Board of Medical Specialties. (Neurology and Psychiatry are certified by the same board.)

American Board	General Certificate
Allergy & Immunology	Allergy & Immunology
Anesthesiology	Anesthesiology
Colon & Rectal Surgery	Colon & Rectal Surgery
Dermatology	Dermatology
Emergency Medicine	Emergency Medicine
Family Practice	Family Practice
Internal Medicine	Internal Medicine
Medical Genetics	Clinical Biochemical Genetics
	Clinical Biochemical/Molecular Genetics
	Clinical Genetics
	Clinical Cytogenics
	Ph.D. Medical Genetics
Neurological Surgery	Neurological Surgery
Nuclear Medicine	Nuclear Medicine
Obstetrics & Gynecology	Obstetrics & Gynecology

Ophthalmology	Ophthalmology
Orthopedic Surgery	Orthopedic Surgery
Otolaryngology	Otolaryngology
Pathology	Anatomic & Clinical Pathology
	Anatomic Pathology
	Clinical Pathology
Pediatrics	Pediatrics
Physical Medicine & Rehabilitation	Physical Medicine & Rehabilitation
Plastic Surgery	Plastic Surgery
Preventive Medicine	Aerospace Medicine
	Occupational Medicine
	Public Health & General Preventive Medicine
Psychiatry & Neurology	Psychiatry
	Neurology
	Neurology with Special Qualifications in Child Neurology
Radiology	Radiology
	Diagnostic Radiology
	Radiation Oncology
	Therapeutic Radiology
	Radiological Physics
Surgery	Surgery
Thoracic Surgery	Thoracic Surgery
Urology	Urology

INDEX

ABOUT THE AUTHOR

SUE BERKMAN is a health writer whose special interest is "service": helping health care consumers find a better way. She has coauthored books on health, and her articles have appeared in many national magazines. She lives and works on a farm in Amenia, New York.